FLY FISHING
the SOLITUDE
Montana

RIVERBEND
PUBLISHING

text and photography by **Trapper Badovinac**

Acknowledgements

Special thanks to Mark Lewis for the wonderful illustrations; to Craig Podner, Ron Pierce, Joleen Tadej, and all the other helpful people at Montana Fish, Wildlife & Parks; to my brother Mark for lending his help on many of the photography shoots; and, a very special thanks to my wife Shirley for her patience and expert design in the production of this book.

FRONT COVER: *Stu Kirkpatrick finds his own fly fishing solitude on the North Fork of the Blackfoot.*

BACK COVER:

TOP: *Westslope cutthroat are the predominant trout species on high-country streams.*

MIDDLE: *A Deer Hair Caddis serves to imitate both the caddis and the smaller stoneflies.*

BOTTOM: *Caddisflies are the predominant aquatic insects on these streams.*

AUTHOR PHOTO: *John Reddy Photography (www.johnreddyphoto.com)*

Book design by Shooting Star Publications.
Illustrations page 10, 11, 12, 56, 57, and 59 by Mark Lewis.

Cataloging-in-Publication data is on file at the Library of Congress.

ISBN 1-931832-67-6
Text and photography © 2006 Trapper Badovinac
© 2006 Riverbend Publishing

For more information about our books write Riverbend Publishing, P. O. Box 5833, Helena, MT 59604; call (866) 787-2363; or visit http://www.riverbendpublishing.com.

Created, produced, and designed in the United States. Printed in South Korea.

10 09 08 07   SI   2 3 4 5

Table of Contents

Foreword

As a child I would regularly fall asleep with a Zane Gray or Louis L'Amour novel. Drifting off, I'd become the hero of those books. There I was, next to a campfire, coffee cup in hand, leaning against my saddle, as I pensively gazed into the flames, planning how I would rescue the town and win the girl. At first I rescued the girl because all the cowboys in the books did, but I really didn't see the point. Later I discovered why that was important.

Sometimes I'd watch western movies at the Saturday afternoon matinee, but often, when the cowboys were near a stream, I'd drift away from the main plot of the movie, wondering if there were trout darting away as the men rode their horses through perfectly good fishing holes.

Turned loose for the summer, my friend Griz and I rode our trusty Schwinns down dusty roads in search of adventure. It didn't take us long to realize that fantasy was much more glamorous than reality. Sleeping on the ground next to a campfire with only a thin Army-surplus blanket was so uncomfortable it fell under the "cruel and unusual punishment" clause of the 8th Amendment. Cooking on a campfire singed most of one eyebrow that fell into our pot of beanie-weenies. That didn't matter much since our grub was so burnt you could hardly taste the eyebrow. It didn't take us long to realize that while we yearned for adventure, we really wanted it without the pain-in-the-ass factor.

I still fantasize about the adventure of exploration but now I'm more likely to follow these mental pursuits as I fall asleep in my pre-bed chair reading destination articles about great trout water. I've learned a lot since Griz and I made the West safe for civilized folks. I've learned that if you do it right, you can go off to explore, fish, and then return home or to camp to a really nice single malt scotch, a great dinner, and a bed without rocks boring holes in your vertebrae.

Sometimes though, it seems that there's nothing new left for me to explore besides outer space or my feminine side – neither of which is very likely. I remember my history lessons where we memorized how Christopher Columbus discovered America in 1492. After closer examination I realized that he was so lost he didn't just miss his exit, he was on the wrong continent. In addition, there were all these Indians there to greet him. It seemed obvious to me that they weren't going to share any of their secret fishing spots with him, much less information about which patterns were working best.

I began to realize that in order to fulfill my explorer/adventurer needs I didn't have to find a trout stream that no one had ever seen before. I just had to find streams that were new to me and hadn't seen more foot traffic than a college campus.

I set off to find and fish the solitude. What I discovered were my beloved small streams.

When I hear the whir of the dentist's drill, I close my eyes and walk the path down to moving water. I can hear my wading boots crush the mint that releases its sweet fragrance. Like a great wine, its aroma is an announcement of astonishing things to come. Then, I'm there. I hear the peaceful rush of water as it tumbles over rock and wood, bending to conform to the shape of the stream. My focus moves to the gentle little runs and holes where trout lurk in the shadows looking for food and where my own imitation will settle in among the ranks of the naturals. Mayflies struggle to fly off the surface and my mind's eye captures that parade of flies as they surf out of the riffle toward the bank, twirling in circles like ballerinas dressed as angels. After many years of standing thigh deep in these waters, they have adopted me as their son, and they are always within arm's reach in my thoughts. These little waters are the manna for my soul.

CHAPTER ONE

Navigational and Evaluation Tools

*B*ig cities intimidate me. I wasn't always this way. I lived in Denver and Colorado Springs, Colorado for a time, but I found myself looking at too much concrete and not enough trees so I moved to Montana.

I once watched the TV show "Fear Factor." I've fished through enough hatches where bugs were crawling up my nose and behind my sunglasses that eating the cockroaches wouldn't bother me much. And I've filled my waders and got pulled downstream enough times to not panic while diving for the underwater flags. Put me in a tank full of eels and my heart rate would barely beat above resting levels. But after years of living in my little house in western Montana, the fear of driving in a big city to get to the place where they'd film that show would make me want to vomit across my dashboard.

An engineer with a belly full of bourbon likely laid out San Francisco streets. Or maybe they followed old cow trails. Then add in the hills, thousands of cars, and pedestrians. You've just engineered the perfect tourist nightmare. There are wonderful little surprises like when you drive north on Highway 101 it changes from five lanes to two and suddenly you're at a stoplight in Chinatown. You can see the top of the Golden Gate Bridge but you're asked to follow some moonbeam to maneuver through all the one-way streets. It makes you want to park your car and walk. But then you'd discover

Equipped with all the high-country essentials, Kerry Eberhart savors the rewards of catching native westslope cutthroat trout on the North Fork of the Blackfoot River.

the nearest parking spot is 150 miles away in Modesto, and you have to use a credit card to pay for a day's parking because the cash you'd need would settle the national debt of Brazil.

It was a November day, and I was deeply embedded in the bowels of downtown San Francisco doing a book signing and fly-tying demonstration at Leland's Fly Fishing Outfitter. This is a wonderful fly-fishing store with staff so fun and knowledgeable that I'd put them up against any store in the country. Looking at all the great gear and photos of the Smith River made me feel like I had found a familiar spot in an alien universe that was

Finding your own fishing spot has plenty of rewards but requires some basic knowledge of the backcountry.

devoid of stars in the night sky. The constant flow of people in and out of the store was very impressive. Men in $2,000 Armani suits and shoes with leather tassels conversed freely about hackle and dubbing. Women dressed like movie stars were standing right in front of me, asking me about Trico hatches and reach casts. Where I live in rural Montana, women dress up by pulling their hair back and putting on a pair of jeans that don't smell like alfalfa and manure.

It was time to leave even though the wine and cheese tasting was just getting started. After a pit stop I headed for the door, making my goodbyes, when Kevin, a staff member, stopped me.

"Where are you going?" Kevin asked.

"Down to Mountain View to visit my good friend Jim Kelly," I replied.

"Now?" His voice carried an incredulous tone, like I had just told him I was going to swim to Honolulu in the dark.

"Sure, why not?" I asked, trying to be calm, but slowly looking over his shoulder expecting to see a hostage negotiation in progress.

"Have you looked outside?" Kevin turned so that I could get a clear view of their storefront window. I anticipated the orange glow of a mushroom cloud but all I saw was fading light and cars parked in the street.

"Kevin, why are all those cars parked in the street?" His self-restraint was amazing. His reply was two words:

"Rush hour."

Fear really begins in the pit of your stomach. I had it all planned out that I could find my way through all the buildings and traffic if I just had some sunlight to act as a navigational beacon. Now, my beacon was gone, and I was going to have to rely on that misty moonbeam again for guidance. As near panic set in I remained outwardly calm while secretly plotting to kidnap Kevin and force him to accompany me and act as my guide in this frightening wilderness.

Later, with step-by-step instructions and a map downloaded and printed from their computer, I set off. First I had to part-out my oldest grandson to pay for the all-day parking, but then I was off on my adventure through the maze of downtown San

Francisco, in the dark, both metaphorically and otherwise. Between the map and Kevin's directions "sort of a half left at the stop light" I suddenly found myself on the freeway but the traffic moved at about the same speed as the city streets so it was hard to tell. After a couple of hours I arrived at my destination, a scant 50 miles from where I started. The woman at the hotel desk was speaking with an accent I'd never heard before, but she understood "Visa" and I understood "room key."

Clearly out of my element, I needed help to find my way around. It was a daunting experience. But with a map, advice from the locals, and some knowledge of where I was and where I wanted to be, I soon found myself getting around like a local – moving so slow my speedometer needle barely moved and talking on my cell phone.

When you make the decision to fish little known waters, one of the first things you'll have to learn is how to find and evaluate a stream. Looking at maps and doing research before you ever leave the comfort of your home can save you time and eliminate frustration when you arrive at the new water. Maps, particularly topographic maps, are an invaluable resource to the fly fisher.

Personal navigators or using Global Positioning System (GPS) receivers are a high-tech way of navigating. Many of these units have the ability to move topo maps to and from a personal computer.

The Basics

Getting lost can turn the best day of fly fishing into a nightmare if you have to spend a cold, hungry night in the woods. Obviously people found their way through the woods long before Global Positioning Satellites or even a rudimentary compass. All this information has been written about in great detail in books, magazines, and Internet articles. There are outdoor courses available where you can learn all the details of navigation. Before you venture off into the woods, take the time to check out at least some of these resources.

Anything man-made will eventually be broken, lost, or run out

In addition to your favorite rod, it's prudent to include essential navigational tools such as a compass and topographic map.

of batteries at the most crucial time. Know that the very best tool you have available will always be the one between your ears. Our human ability to reason and process information given to the brain through the senses will always be superior to any other instrument.

The sun, moon, and stars have been used for navigation since ancient times. There are other things that exist in nature that can also act as guides to direction. In the Rocky Mountain West the large vistas and open space assist orientation. If you're standing on the top of a mountain and can see your vehicle, knowing which direction you need to go is pretty simple. If you get out of your vehicle and fish your way upstream, finding your way back can be as simple as following the stream back to your car. These are common-sense rules and when things occur as expected, everything is fine.

However, days in the woods rarely go exactly as planned and it's wise to have some foundational knowledge to safely guide you back to where you want to go. The Rocky Mountains are basically a semi-arid environment, and the elevations on average are higher than those in the east. This means that hillsides facing south get cooked in the sun much more than those on the north-

IF YOU BECOME LOST

If you become lost, the first rule of business is to use your head instead of your feet. Sit on a log or rock, take several deep breaths, and think. If you left your vehicle that morning and fished your way upstream, you should be able to easily return by reversing your route, using the stream as a guide.

If you've moved away from the stream for some reason and can't find your way back, the solution becomes more complicated. You're without a map, compass, GPS, or other tools, the temperature is dropping, and it's beginning to rain. Your raincoat, matches, water, and food are in the car. Panic is setting in as the sun drops low and the shadows lengthen. What do you do?

- If you brought a cell phone, give it a try.
- Build a fire.
- If you are with someone else, or your dog, stay together. You'll be easier to find and you'll need each other for warmth.
- Stay warm and dry. Next to panic, hypothermia is your biggest enemy.
- Stay in one place. Search-and-rescue teams move very slowly looking for clues. If you are moving very quickly ahead of them, they won't find you until you stop.
- Find a comfortable place to wait. An ideal place would be out of the wind and/or rain, but don't lie on the ground as this can rob your body heat.
- Put out a very visible or bright object.
- Don't eat anything you're not certain about. Hunger is uncomfortable but people can and do survive for many days without food.
- If you brought water or a filter bottle (see Chapter 3) use it to stay hydrated. If not, you may have to improvise by finding a spring, stream, or even the dew from leaves, depending on how long you are lost and the weather conditions.
- A small whistle is useful to alert rescuers or other nearby hikers or anglers.

facing slopes. The result is less trees and vegetation on south-facing slopes. Use this information on a smaller scale by looking at snow melting on rocks. Even if there is little direct sun, the snow on rocks will melt faster on the sides facing south. If there has been a recent rain, the rocks will dry on the south side first. Keep in mind that these are all rules of thumb and not absolutes. You can have a south-facing slope that is potted with natural springs; it may have more trees than the north-facing slopes in the vicinity. In many areas there is enough moisture that the trees on both slopes are pretty equal.

Everyone knows the sun rises in the east and sets in the west. But in July in Montana it rises in the northeast and sets in the northwest. In January it rises in the southeast and sets in the southwest.

Learn to orient yourself. Be observant and check out your surroundings. Get curious as hell.

At night, if you find the Big Dipper and look at the cup portion, the two outside stars will point to the North Star (Polaris) that is on the end of the handle of the Little Dipper. Visually multiply the space between the two Big Dipper stars times six and

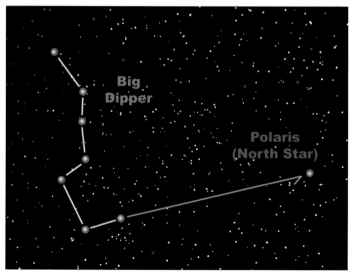

You'll find the Big Dipper in the northern night sky. By multiplying the distance between the stars on the outside of the cup by six, you'll find Polaris.

that gives you the distance to Polaris. Another tip is to align the tips of a crescent moon and it points roughly south.

From these and other simple, rudimentary signs in nature you should be able to determine north even in the dark. Hopefully, when you left your vehicle that morning, you took a few minutes to orient yourself so that knowing where north is will actually do you some good.

We fly fishers tend to get fixated. Our universe shrinks to the distance between us and those rising fish. If you are in an unfamiliar place, take the time to look around. Pick out landmarks such as rockslides or anything a little bit out of the ordinary. Every hour or so, stop and ask yourself which way is the vehicle from your location. When you turn around 180 degrees, the scenery looks much different. This is what it will look like on the return hike. Of course a very simple tool that is inexpensive and lightweight is a compass. If you haven't used that compass to orient yourself when you left the truck, its value is greatly diminished. When search and rescue teams set out to find someone, the first thing they look for is some clue in your vehicle. Finding an empty rod tube would tell them you are probably fishing, but a little note or map about where you planned to go would really cut down the variables as to where they should look for you. They would also check with anyone you might have talked to, like the local ranger or your spouse. Many trailheads have a pencil and check-in sheet. If it only saves your life once, it would be well worth the few minutes it takes to fill it out.

Topographic Maps

Maps and GPS can be used for many more things than just finding your way back to your vehicle. They can aid you in evaluating a stream before you ever go afield.

Maps have a built-in set of problems. The earth is three-dimensional and spherical. Maps are two-dimensional rectangles. It would have been a whole lot easier if the earth had been flat! Carefully peel an orange with the fewest number of pieces of peel, and then reassemble them and try to flatten it. You will

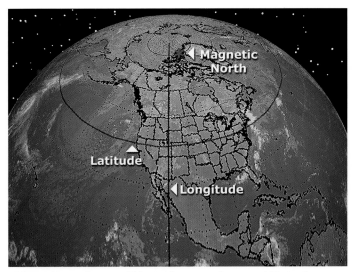

If the earth were flat it would be much easier to draw maps! Having basic map reading skills will allow you to safely find your way.

immediately see the problem. Since you have this orange already peeled, notice the vertical lines formed by the segments. In map lingo these are longitude. Latitude lines run parallel to the equator and perpendicular to the longitude. Since longitude runs to the poles it would seem that north would be easy to find on a map, but unfortunately there are two different 'norths.' True north points to this imaginary intersection, but magnetic north isn't exactly on the intersection of all these imaginary lines, so every topo map shows you how much to correct for this. This is called the angle of declination. A compass needle points to magnetic north, but deposits of iron ore can sometimes give you a false reading.

Topographic maps, or topos, provide a wealth of information to a fly fisher exploring a new stream. They are a graphic representation of both natural and man-made objects laid out to scale. A small portion of the earth is shown using contour lines to display both the steepness as well as the shape of the terrain. The United States Geological Survey (USGS) is the main distributor of topo maps, and most outdoor stores have maps for their local area. When choosing a map, look at all the information at the

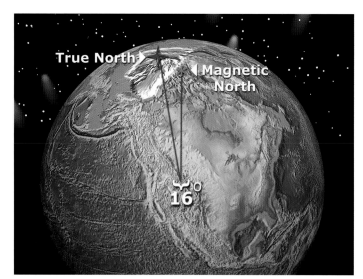

A compass will point to magnetic north, while longitudinal lines run to true north. Knowing the declination angle is imperative.

bottom to determine its scale and other data to make sure you have chosen the right one(s) for the area you'll be fishing. Often times you'll need to purchase more than one if the trip you choose goes outside the boundary of the map. The 7.5-minute (7.5') maps are the most detailed and the most popular. They cover an area that is 7.5' of latitude and 7.5' of longitude. One very important piece of data is called the contour interval. This tells you how many feet of elevation each interval line represents. Simply put, if the lines are close together, it's steeper; further apart it's flatter. Many people purchase some sort of GPS receiver with the mistaken thought that they can safely go into the woods with nothing else. But topos let you study an area before your visit to make judgments about where you might want to fish and areas you may want to avoid. For example, if you looked at a topo and saw that a stream went through a narrow and steep canyon, you might very well avoid that section of the stream. The contour lines of the topo give you a three-dimensional view of the land. The lines on a 7.5-minute map will typically be at 40-foot intervals. Some GPS receivers can display topo maps downloaded from your PC, but I've never seen a hardcopy topo map run out of batteries or be

rendered useless after falling in the water. Map lamination is available but now you can also buy waterproof paper and print out what you'd like on your computer's printer. Topo maps, when used with a good compass, are the most reliable navigational method available.

Using Topos to Locate Potential Streams

Water temperature is crucial to trout fisherman because it is crucial to trout; too cold or too warm and the fish become inactive. Trout have survived millions of years by adhering to their instincts and wild trout especially are very tuned to water temperatures. There have been studies where hatchery trout were put in an artificial run of very cold water. Some actively fed on the food sporadically supplied by the biologists; some ignored the food and retreated to slower water. In the end, those who fed lost more body weight than those who ate nothing because they expended more calories than they were able to ingest.

When looking for good trout water on a freestone stream, consider what time of the year you'll likely be fishing the area. During periods of snowmelt and spring run-off, the water will be colder. You'll want to find areas where the water is warmed by the sun. This usually means slower moving water or areas with greater sun exposure. Shadowed canyons and areas of dense overhanging trees will prevent the sun from warming the water.

Normally the further downstream you move, the warmer the water. Study the topo and measure the drop in elevation. Look at the contour lines to determine if the area flows through a canyon. Consider if the area faces south or north, as the south-facing areas will warm more quickly. Use the map to find clues about factors that effect water temperature. Simply put, sunshine, slow moving water or standing water, and hot springs increase water temperatures, while shade, glaciers, springs, and fast moving water decreases the temperature.

Intermittent streams are normally indicated on topos with a broken blue line. Look at the map's legend for the exact symbol.

Knowing many of a stream's characteristics such as gradient and path will answer some questions but not all. If a stream runs through a stand of dense trees, very little sunlight will hit the water. This will dramatically slow the aquatic insect activity and the dry fly fishing.

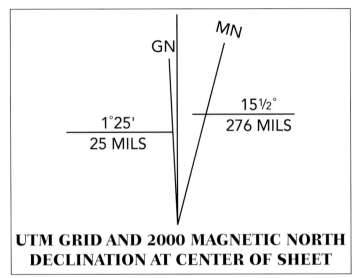

It is very important to find and understand the map details that appear on all USGS topo maps. Use the declination data to find north.

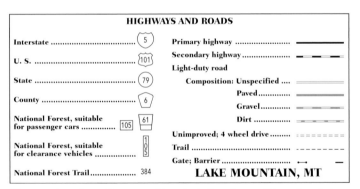

The map legend provides many things including the condition of roads from paved to 4-wheel-drive only.

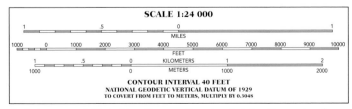

Scale is very crucial in judging distances. Keep in mind that distance is only one element. Add in terrain gradient when evaluating any hike.

Intermittent streams are not normally very productive water because they dry up during the heat of the summer and in drought years may have little if any flow. But what often isn't considered are streams that flow through farm or ranch country where huge amounts of water are pumped out during dry years. These sections of rivers face several challenges.

The Montana Fish, Wildlife & Parks Department has been working with farmers and ranchers to change several things to benefit both the trout streams and the landowners. One huge problem is something as simple as a culvert. Normally when ranchers build roads over a small stream, they rarely use bridges, as they are costly to build and maintain. A simple solution is a culvert, and for the rancher, the smaller the culvert, the less the cost. Culverts that are too small create water velocity that trout cannot swim through or around because there is too much water forced through too small an area. In nature, it's rare that a narrow slot of rocks would be so uniform that it offered no places for the fish to leap over. A man-made culvert can stop fish from moving upstream to spawn. A practical solution is either a bridge or a larger diameter culvert that allows easy water movement without denying the rancher access to his property.

Livestock need water and can cause considerable degradation to the stream by breaking down banks and destroying the fragile riparian habitat. Ranchers who bring water to a trough set back from the stream protect both the stream and the plant life needed to hold the banks together.

Irrigation pumps pull water from the stream and deliver it to the field. Fish often get pulled into the system and are left to die. There are ingenious devices to separate the fish and wood debris from the irrigation water. The rancher is happy and the fish are returned to the stream.

All these issues plus many more are at play when a trout stream runs through an agricultural area. All of them can affect the health of a trout stream. A topo map can show you where these areas are but can't really tell you much about the operation of the individual landowner. While there are Geographic Information System mapping studies being done that could provide contact information for these ranchers, these are far from complete and the only way to know for certain is to visit the area. For Montana, going to www.nris.state.mt.us/gis/ownmaps.asp will provide some information.

Use the map legend to determine what is privately owned land, Bureau of Land Management (BLM), National Forest (NF), State Forest, or designated Wilderness. Often, there are roads near the stream of interest and if both are on any public land, many of the agricultural issues are rendered moot. Montana has over 30 million acres of public land, which is roughly the size of Mississippi. While all of it is open for fly fishing, not all has a road through it or is easily accessible without some hiking.

Look for the campground symbols. Equestrians use many campgrounds in Montana, especially those adjacent to wilderness areas. The streams near these campgrounds are often lightly fished, and as a bonus you'll find well-defined and maintained horse trails. Find these trails on the topo map to determine if they follow the stream of interest. Walking these trails, even if they stray for a time from the stream, normally provides a safe and relatively easy passage. These trails often follow the contour lines through a canyon, thus avoiding a lot of hill climbing. This is easier on the horse and easier for the walk-in fly fisherman. Bears and other animals and horseback riders will also use these trails, so stay alert. When actively navigating by way of a horse trail, it makes finding your location on a topo map much easier; you will only need to determine at what point on the trail you are currently standing.

Water issues in the Rocky Mountains are crucial and water is bought, stolen, or traded frequently. The civil courts are inundated with lawsuits about water rights and it's an issue that is destined to only get worse as more people make more demands on the resource. Fish often end up at the end of the request line and their only voice is that of the trout fisherman.

When considering water factors, look where the stream originates and what feeds it. Streams that begin in wilderness areas will be untouched by anything man-made until they leave that safe haven. Snowpack, particularly in higher elevations, acts like a frozen reservoir as it releases water from a solid to a liquid over time. In Montana, many high-country areas have snow all but a few weeks out of the year. This provides an almost year-round source for a stream except during drought years. Small lakes and springs are also good signs that cold constant water is available to a stream.

Intermittent sources of water adversely affect the aquatic insects that trout feed on. If the stream dries up, the insect larvae will die and fish populations will suffer.

By scouting a stream using the various methods described here, when you finally arrive at the stream you'll have more time to enjoy it.

The structure in or near a river can rarely be learned by any method other than first-hand observation. On Monture Creek deadfalls provide perfect shelter for trout.

Mining and timber operations have been a part of Montana culture for a very long time. Until recently, fish have been ignored when jobs were at stake. Now huge cleanup efforts are under way to reverse the pollution sins of the past. But many mines have been long abandoned by companies that no longer exist, even though their tailing piles continue to leach heavy metals into the rivers and streams. These heavy metals move through the food chain and end up in the brain of a trout, dramatically shortening its life. Most of these old mine sites are clearly marked on topo maps, but some very small ones are not. Simply seeing a mine site doesn't necessarily mean the fishing will be bad, but it is a factor to consider. It also might provide a means to search the Internet to see if there have been newspaper articles about the area. There are long sections of the Clark Fork River that are nearly void of fish because of mining and those areas have been the subject of many media reports.

Timber harvesting, particularly clear-cutting, can create a secondary issue for the stream because, without the trees, there may be nothing to stop or even slow down the spring runoff. This often results in a very muddy runoff and can create silting in the substrate that can kill the aquatic insects. No bugs mean no food for the trout. The steeper the terrain, the greater the adverse effect on the stream.

Global Positioning Systems

Recently, some rental car companies have installed sophisticated Global Positioning Systems (GPS) in their cars. The driver simply inputs the destination address and the onboard system displays a map, route, and verbal directions. This sort of technology is a dream come true to people like me who can find their way around large cities but would love to have a local sitting next to us, telling us when to turn, which lane to be in, and where all the traffic jams are likely to be.

You could buy a GPS system like those in some rental cars, plus a laptop with a wireless connection, and a local cab driver sitting next to you monitoring the laptop. Then you could tune

Small GPS receivers like this one from Garmin are great tools. Learn to use them properly and carry a low-tech backup—a compass and map.

the radio to the all news stations for traffic reports and talk to another driver on your cell phone about what's going on up ahead. Then you'd never get lost. That's a lot of technology to be monitoring instead of driving your car. All this high technology is based on low technology – GPS is no exception. Before you venture into the unknown, study and learn how to find your way even if the technology fails you.

I have a Garmin eTrex Personal Navigator. It's a lot of fun and it gives me options – options are good.

GPS was developed with your tax dollars to aid in military navigation. Tanks, planes, ships, and many Humvees use this technology to know where they are in the world. The receiver provides the location by receiving signals from various satellites that orbit the earth. It does a pretty good job as long as there is an unobstructed view of the sky. If you are in a steep canyon or heavy trees it doesn't work well. These little guys eat batteries like a puppy with a plate of unguarded bacon. With the batteries gone, it's a rock with a lanyard attached. Carry extra batteries along with a compass and topo map of the area. The other pitfall of these receivers is not using them correctly. One day I was out fishing with my wife, Shirley, on a small stream near our house. This

Using the Navigate to Waypoint feature of your GPS after climbing out of a steep canyon would likely make your return trip much easier.

stream had a lot of twists and turns with heavy vegetation. I wanted to impress her with my new high-tech toy so I showed her how we could navigate back to the truck with a feature called "Go to Waypoint." The problem was that I mistakenly entered a Waypoint from another stream 25 miles away, so we were navigating to the wrong spot. After about 15 minutes I took the unit from her and looked at it and realized what I had done. I then shut it off and walked back to the truck using my brain instead of the technology. Before you place your health in the hands of these units, become very familiar with the various features and double check what you are looking at on the display. Then, don't ever believe that it can replace your brain, which should also tell you to pack a map and compass.

GPS receivers are relatively inexpensive units. The more features you add, the more complicated it becomes but simply put, when navigating with these units, you establish "Waypoints" and a "track log." Spend some time around your neighborhood or park figuring out how to create, store, and retrieve these with your unit. One of the very first things you'll realize is that it takes a few minutes for the GPS receiver to "acquire" the satellites after you turn it on. Until the unit is functioning properly, its readings are worthless. If you are going to use the unit, turning it on should be the first thing you do after exiting your vehicle. Then, while you're putting on waders, assembling your rod, and loading your vest, the GPS is getting into full-function mode. Most of these units have a signal that alerts you when it is ready. Keep in mind that bad data is worse than no data.

Waypoints (WP)

The WP records and stores your current location. If you venture into new territory it's a good idea to mark a waypoint at the location of your vehicle. When you want to return or reference this location, it's been digitally recorded and saved. This is especially useful if you decide to take a different route back to your starting point instead of step-by-step backtracking along the stream you just fished. Most GPS receivers have a function called "Navigate to WP." This allows you to use the unit much like a homing beacon as it will give you updated course directions, distance to WP, and time, based on your current rate of travel. Most have an arrow on the display that takes the guesswork out of "Which way is back to the car?" The upside of this function is that you don't need to keep the unit powered up during the day, and if your GPS receiver has a topo map function, it will be easy to evaluate the easiest way back. For example, if the closest way back is down a very steep cliff, you would want to go around the cliff, but then follow the arrow pointer to resume your "Navigate to WP" function. WPs are initially recorded as numbers but you can easily edit these to give them relevant names like "NF trailhead." As these units can store hundreds of WPs you wouldn't want to label them with something generic like "road" or "bridge," or something moveable like "car." As you add WPs, over time you won't likely remember just which stream this "road" WP refers to. If you are on Long Lost Creek and set the unit to "Navigate to WP," and the WP is the one you saved on Yur Very Lost Creek, you could end up using the GPS to get horribly lost.

The "Navigate to WP" mode is a course correction function. In order for it to work properly you must be actively traveling on a course. Set the unit to navigate back to the WP you set at your vehicle, and then begin to walk. If you have a clear view of the sky, the directional arrow will point to your car. As you continue to walk the unit will calculate your rate of speed and the distance to the WP.

Track Log

Another function of GPS units is a track log. This is like leaving electronic breadcrumbs on your trail so you can follow them back out. As you travel, the unit records your course along a topo map on the GPS screen. You will need to leave the unit turned on and in a position where the antenna can work properly. All GPS units get their signals from orbiting satellites. If the unit's antenna cannot find the satellite, it cannot function properly. While they can transmit and receive through lighter materials like a shirt pocket, stuffing the GPS into the bottom of your backpack will likely render it useless. It needs a clear path toward the sky.

The newer units have topo map capability built into them. Since they don't have enough memory to hold the entire United States, the map programs are stored on a CD that can be called up on your computer, and then small portions can be downloaded to the GPS receiver. These maps, when viewed on a computer, are great for evaluating streams using everything you read about using topos earlier in this chapter.

Normally while fly fishing, finding your way back is as simple as reversing course and using the stream as your guide.

CHAPTER TWO

Researching the Stream

Advanced research of a stream will save you time, energy, money, and frustration. Just blindly driving to a drainage and then trying to find a place to fish most likely won't prove productive.

Yosemite National Park, as seen through the lens of Ansel Adams, has always intrigued me. Adams' carefully composed photographs were the stuff of legends back in the 1970s when I attended college in California. In 1975 I took a break from my studies and my full-time job to visit this wonderful park. The plan was to spend four days in the area photographing the wonderful landscapes and vistas and from time to time, put down my camera and pick up my old fiberglass rod to cast to rising golden trout on small deserted streams. Reality didn't much match the fantasy.

My "far out" hippy girlfriend Kathy and I arrived at the Yosemite Village campgrounds after a long drive in our packed-to-the-rooftop VW Beetle. She was a California native who knew we needed reservations. That was a major shock to this Colorado boy who was used to stopping along a dirt road and throwing a piece of canvas on the ground to cover my sleeping bag. When we arrived at the park, the line of cars extended back to Merced. The ranger tried to sell us firewood! In my mind this was like selling air. We finally made our way to our campsite or more accurately a parking spot at what looked

Stu Kirkpatrick takes a well deserved break after hiking a few miles into the North Fork of the Blackfoot River.

like a tailgate party at an NFL game. After numerous "Far outs" and "Right ons" we ate our macrobiotic dinner and crawled into our tent for a romantic evening of barking dogs, screaming kids, loud music, and bears turning over trash cans.

By 5:00 A.M. we had the Beetle packed and were on our way to someplace quiet like downtown L.A. We headed east through the park and ended up camped on a little stream in the Tuolumne Meadows area. The flapping of my bellbottom jeans was the only sound as I walked through the woods along this wonderful creek. A large fallen log invited me to sit and finish my beer as I watched small trout take spotted sedge from the surface. Kathy was behind me taking off her bra under her shirt. It always looked like a couple of golden retriever puppies playing under her shirt and then she would, magician like, extract the bra from her shirtsleeve with the requisite announcement, "There, that's better." Hippy girls didn't like bras.

The rest of the afternoon was spent catching small, stocker rainbow trout on a little Bucktail Caddis pattern. The solitude of this small stream healed the wounds of the previous nightmare at the village. Food, cold beer, and Kathy awaited me back at camp and I turned my attention that direction.

The name-calling broke the stillness. The two boys were about eight years old. They had managed to get the little rod and reel off the cardboard backing and assembled, but were struggling with the line on the 49-cent reel as they sat on the creek bank.

"What's the problem, boys?" I asked. They quickly turned toward me and offered up the rod and reel.

"Can you help us mister? We can't get this to work." Their sad eyes were pleading. Who could refuse?

After a few minor adjustments like turning the reel around on the rod, we had hook, line, and sinker ready to go, but no bait. Our search for grubs and worms under various rocks produced enough to keep them busy for a while. After some short casting lessons and a set of rules to determine whose turn it was, they were catching the

Finding your own new "secret spot" is a reward in itself. Some liken it to finding a Christmas present around every new bend.

There are many lightly used streams in the Rocky Mountains that people drive by on their way to the big-named rivers.

Most fly fishers equate small streams with small fish. This beautiful rainbow trout took a dry fly on a stream most people write off as not worth their effort.

small rainbows. When I suggested that they release the fish back into the stream they looked at me much like my own father did when I made the same suggestion to him – like I was suggesting we give back free ice cream cones at Baskin Robbins. The shouts of their glee and "I got one!" faded as I made my way back to camp. Kathy was there chatting with a Buick-sized woman wearing a sweat-stained tank top that exposed part of her industrial-strength bra. Her companion was an equally large pear-shaped man who sat next to her at the picnic table, listening to a radio. He alternated his attention between the ball game and Kathy's well-filled and recently laundered tank top. Upon my arrival he quickly turned around at the table.

"Did you see two small boys?" The woman asked. She seemed pleasant enough.

"Yeah," I answered. "They were busy fishing."

"That'll keep 'em busy," radio man said without looking up.

I popped a beer and sat on the ground strategically upwind of Bubba and Wanda. Kathy joined me by lying on her back with her head on my thigh. Her long brown hair was braided into an interwoven maze with a daisy to accent it.

My fourth beer was punishing my kidneys when the boys marched out of the woods like tribesman returning to the village with their bounty. Grinning ear-to-ear they carried what must have been 60 or 70 small trout on a 5-foot long stick that ran through the gills of the fish.

The look on the fat man's face was priceless. He jumped up like he'd just heard last call at the all-you-can-eat buffet. "Holy shit! Where'd you get all those fish?"

"We caught 'em," the oldest boy replied, like that wasn't obvious.

"But how?" he asked. It was obvious he never expected the cheap, shrink-wrapped fishing package to do anything but keep the young boys away from his ball game.

"That man showed us," piped the younger one.

Kathy looked at me and the tears were welling up in her eyes. "That was so sweet," she said with a look that let me know that tonight was going to be a really great night. Watching the joy and pride of the boys was reward enough for me but I wasn't going to turn down the bonus round.

The unexpected delights of small streams make really great memories. Prior to the memories comes the research and evaluation.

Stream Evaluation

After learning to read a topo map, and after you've researched the stream using the previous methods, you can refine your search with a second-pass evaluation on an unknown stream.

Internet

The Internet is a great tool for getting all sorts of information about a particular fishery. The state of Montana's propeller heads have done a great job of helping fly fishers all over the world find places to fish. Sometimes figuring out how to sift through all that data to find what you're really looking for is daunting.

The built-in problem is that the Internet is evolving and changing at a mind-boggling rate. If I were to tell you of a fly shop where you could get current information about a particular river, that would be good to know. I could tell the name of the shop, the address and phone number and maybe even the name of someone who would answer your questions. Even if the employee I told you about was gone, or even if the shop changed owners and its name, it's likely the building would still be there. That's not necessarily true with the Internet. I could give you the website address where great information is available and tomorrow it could be gone, "poof" – evaporated into the ether-neverlands of the web. Commercial websites can be very transient; government sites tend to be more stable. The best solution is to learn how to navigate around the web.

There are Internet sites out there that can give you all sorts of data from maps that show the boundaries of public and private land, how many fishermen user days by year, roads, campgrounds, and nearby towns. The problem lies with telling you how to find such a site. By the time the ink is dry on this book, the site may have a different name, or provide different data, or have a different address. Instead, I'll tell you how to find it by doing a search. I'm not a hi-tech guru, but I can lead you through this maze if you've never been here before.

When a website is made, the person making it wants people to visit the site. Invisible to the user are a series of keywords that the author believes people will use to try and find his type of site. Words like "fishing" or "guide" would likely be keywords used on an outfitter's website.

A search engine is a website that takes your keywords and then searches the Internet for matches. One search engine is called Google. If you type: *Google.com* in the line of your computer application designed for inputting website addresses, after a few seconds a window will open. Inside this window you'll find a blank box. It is here where you'll type in the keywords. Each search engine has rules for how you can best use its site. It's good

Fishing the Internet isn't as much fun as casting to rising fish on Cottonwood Creek.

to read through these simple rules, as they normally are accompanied by examples. But basically the more precise you are, the better the results. If, for example, you typed in: *fishing* and then clicked on the search button, you would get a list of millions of websites, too many to look through in a lifetime. Typing in: *"Cottonwood Creek" + Montana* will list merely thousands of websites. One of the rules is that putting quote marks around a phrase tells the software to look for where these words appear together just like you typed them. The "+" sign means that the next word also must appear somewhere in the text. So if we assume that there is a Cottonwood Creek in just about every state, adding in Montana will simplify things. Adding more specific words will help even more. Typing in: *"Cottonwood Creek" + Montana + guide + "fly fishing"* will narrow the search down to a couple of hundred.

There's another way. Each state, including Montana, has a website. There is a convention or rule for all 50 states. It is this: www.state.nn.us.

Here, "nn" is the two-letter abbreviation for each state. So Montana would be: www.state.mt.us.

This will take you to the Montana state website. As you explore this website you should be able to find information about fishing, tourism, or recreation.

Each state has a department that deals with fishing, hunting and outdoor recreation and it has a website of its own. In Montana that state agency is called Fish, Wildlife & Parks (FWP). Within the FWP website is a Fishing Guide that is very useful. You can look up different rivers, lakes, or streams and you'll find maps that show private and public property. That website is currently: fwp.state.mt.us/fishing/guide/default.aspx.

Here's the disclaimer – these site addresses change. While this is a state site and it's unlikely that it will go away completely, it could easily be called something else before I finish writing this paragraph. I offer this as an example, but the means to find this information is what's important. It goes back to the old saying, "Give a man a fish and you feed him for a day. Teach a man to fish and you get rid of him for a weekend."

Within the bowels of the Internet, you can likely discover enough information about a stream to know whether it's viable or not. But there are many streams in Montana that won't be listed under this site for various reasons. Often a low-tech solution is needed to augment what you've found.

Besides the payoff of finding where to fish, the Internet and other information sources can give you foreknowledge of hatches and patterns.

Fly Shops

Local fly shops around an area will often give you mixed results. Most shops in Montana are open seasonally and operate on a very thin profit margin. If you happen to call when an employee is busy working with a customer, it's unlikely he'll ignore the guy with an open checkbook to give you free information about some of his favorite secret fishing spots. The best solution is to visit the shop in person and say something like, "I enjoy fishing smaller streams. Can you sell me some flies that will work and then direct me to one of these streams?" It's a fair trade. If you have researched a stream or two in the area, try pulling out a topo and ask the local guy which one would be the best option and if he has any information on them. Fly shops in Montana are varied. All have a small window of time to make enough profit to sustain them through the rest of the year. During the off season (December-March), or even the shoulder months (October-November, April-May), the employees may be happy to spend time talking about out-of-the-way fishing spots but ignore you during the often frantic times of mid-summer.

Guides and Outfitters

Fishing outfitters in Montana are regulated. They are required to designate certain areas that they operate in and are prohibited from working outside those areas. Most guide from drift boats or rafts, and few do walk and wade trips on a consistent basis. Guides in Montana are mostly independent contractors to the outfitters. After guiding for years, I was frequently asked by clients for information about a smaller stream where they could get away from the big-name rivers to fish in a secluded stream without a guide. This presented a dilemma to me. To give them more than general information, I'd have to provide them with a topo map. Normally they didn't have the correct gear to fish the smaller streams, and I worried about them getting lost. I felt a loyalty to the outfitter who didn't make any money when his clients were fishing on their own and more than a little hesitation about sending people with unknown backcountry skills into uninhabited areas of this state. I

have, however, guided people on walk and wade trips on small streams, but it is by far the exception rather than the rule as most people aren't willing to pay the daily guide fees for this sort of adventure. But, a guided trip on a small Montana stream is possible and some outfitters are happy to provide this service.

Topo Maps

This subject has been covered in the previous chapter, but what you learned from reading topo maps can greatly assist in your evaluation process. Looking at the map in either the electronic or paper version, consider the following:

Does the stream flow into a larger stream or lake? Trout cannot successfully spawn in the still water of lakes and will migrate into tributaries to spawn. Some choose to stay in the tributaries but in years of drought may migrate back to the lake. Streams that are lake fed usually have higher concentrations of fish as they are less susceptible to drought. Many streams in the Blackfoot River drainage, four of which are covered in greater detail later in this

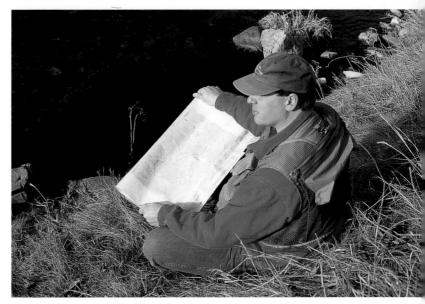

As you study a topo map, look for the many clues that tell you that a stream is viable, such as being fed by a lake or even a glacier.

book, connect to the Big Blackfoot River. The Blackfoot flows into the Clark Fork River, which in turn flows through a series of lakes and streams to eventually empty into the Columbia River and then on to the Pacific Ocean.

Trout migrate from summer runs where they bulk up with plentiful food sources, to wintering areas where they expend minimal amounts of energy and to spawning grounds. Rainbows and cutthroats migrate up the smaller tributaries to spawn each spring. Browns, bull trout, and brookies migrate and spawn in the fall. If migration paths are blocked, the number of fish will often decline. Look for any man-made or natural barriers or dams. Sometime large-scale commercial livestock businesses or com-

mercial ventures will employ diversion dams to draw huge amounts of water that can leave fish stranded. In Chapter One this is explored in greater detail. Not all ranches have these problems, but it's a consideration worth investigating.

The last examination deals with the terrain. Does the stream meander through mostly flat areas? This could mean higher amounts of silt on the bottom or high water temperatures during the summer. The topo map could indicate a wetland where willows and other vegetation might make fly fishing a bit tougher in the dense vegetation. A close examination of the contour lines might show that the terrain is too steep to access safely. If the stream flows through steep canyons, it might be inaccessible to the angler. If the elevation drops too suddenly it could indicate big waterfalls that would create a natural barrier to fish migration and tough going for the fly fisherman.

State Biology Studies

Whirling disease (WD) has adversely affected many great trout streams in the western mountain states. The silver lining is that both tax dollars and private contributions have flowed into the research pockets of fishery biologists that work in state agencies. In order to study the effects of this waterborne disease, biologists use a variety of scientific methods. One particularly interesting to the angler in search of new water is electro-shocking. While this method of surveying fish has been around for many years, its use has been stepped up to determine the effects of WD on fish populations within a given watershed.

On small streams this equipment consists of a portable backpack by which an electrical current is generated. The fish biologist puts the probes into the water and fish are momentarily stunned. They are then counted, measured, and often scales are taken for later testing, including a test for WD. The Montana Fish, Wildlife & Parks Department employees also spend some of their time looking at spawning migration because WD is most devastating to young salmanoids. All this data is collected and then published. These studies show the number of trout per

All states have jumped on the high-tech bandwagon, and data about trout migration and water temperatures are now available online. This data will augment what you find on the stream.

Besides data on water flows and temperatures, state biologists study and report on trout populations, species, and size.

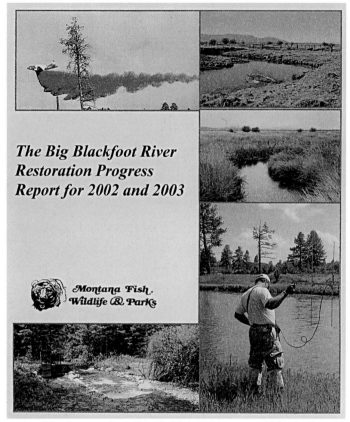

The Big Blackfoot River Restoration Progress Report for 2002 and 2003

Montana Fish, Wildlife & Parks

Reports like this one about the Blackfoot River contain all kinds of useful information to the fly-fishing angler. The title may not be what you expected.

100 feet of stream. Often they show the reader where the fish are, in what concentrations, during different times of the year and what size and species they are. A team of experts who write it up in a neat little report has done much of your research of a stream. Finding these reports can be a bit tricky because the primary purpose of the study is biological instead of being geared toward the curious angler. In the state library I found one for the Blackfoot River drainage entitled "The Big Blackfoot River Restoration Progress Report for 2002 and 2003." While this report gave me everything I was looking for, I initially passed over it because the title didn't strike me as being relevant.

The Report

The data collected for this report is amazing in its thoroughness. It contains water temperatures for 44 tributaries to the Blackfoot River over the entire year. Because hatches are linked to water temperature, and fish activity slows dramatically when water temperatures are too high (> ~70°) or too low (< ~45°), this is very valuable information. You can quickly learn, for example, that in an average year fishing the upper reaches of the Blackfoot River with dry flies before early May isn't going to be very productive.

Fishing the lower reaches of the Blackfoot at mid-day during July isn't going to be all that great either. You'd quickly see that Nevada Spring Creek, which flows slowly through open range to the Blackfoot River, hits a fish-killing 80 degrees in July. Then, if you flip over to the electro-shocking data charts, you find that the biologists captured only one fish over four inches long in 100 feet of this stream.

This sort of data will save any angler many hours of wasted effort on non-productive water.

Some of the electro-shocking data is difficult to evaluate precisely without some first-hand experience. The results are divided up by species captured for both trout and non-trout, then by

Rick Oie fishes the North Fork of the Blackfoot near where it infuses the main stem of the Blackfoot River with much needed cold water.

length. There is a column that gives totals per 100 feet of stream. Without knowing the size of the stream, it's difficult to determine if any stream is worth the effort.

Let's look at the Missouri River in Montana below Holter Dam. This is a famous blue-ribbon trout stream. Tailwaters will normally have much larger populations than freestone rivers. The trout are pampered by gradually changing water temperatures and flows. In 2001, the Missouri River had a near-constant flow of 3,000 +/- 300 cubic feet per second (cfs) discharging from Holter Dam. When a fish count study was conducted that year, the FWP biologists found 1,332 brown trout over 10 inches long per mile in a section of river near the dam. They also found 4,320 rainbow trout over 10 inches long per mile in that same section for a total of 5,652. The average is 3,485. That's a lot of catchable trout and the fishing that year was amazing. In 1998, a high water year, the flow from Holter Dam was near 30,000 cfs at times. The Missouri River is about 100 yards across in places with depths down to about 40 feet.

The Blackfoot is a freestone river in the Columbia River drainage. The median flow on the Blackfoot is roughly 1,000 cfs. It's home to rainbows, browns, westslope cutthroat, and bull trout. In May of 2002, on a lower section of the river, FWP biologists found 132 trout greater than six inches long per 1,000 feet.

To compare the two rivers, I first found a common denominator of 100 feet of river because the Missouri count was done on a per mile basis and the Blackfoot on a per 1000 feet basis. The average count per 100 feet on the Missouri was 67. The average count on the Blackfoot was 13.2. Factoring in the flow differences, because the

Often various federal and state agencies will install monitors and other hardware onto bridges. This one is used to pump water for fighting fires, but some bridges have flow-gauge stations.

Missouri has three times the water flow as the Blackfoot, the advantage still went to the Missouri River tailwater at 22.3 trout >10"/100' vs. 13.2 trout >6"/100' for the Blackfoot.

Of course, there are many other factors involved that could affect your fishing results. For example, brown trout tend to feed when the light is lower if all other conditions are equal. If you like to fish in the middle of sunny days, and you are fishing a stream where the predominant species is browns, the number of fish per mile won't be reflected in your fish count.

The size and flow of a stream must be factored in to the number and size of the trout that reside there. Most large rivers and even some smaller streams have gauge stations on them. This data is fed, via satellite, to the U.S. Geological Survey website, where it is available to the public.

Most small stream flows are not monitored and just looking at a topo map will only reveal approximate sizes of streams. However, if you follow the stream you are evaluating down to a larger river, you can make some rough estimates. Throwing out

A stream with a real-time gauge station provides incomplete information. Knowing the width of the river is another vital element to evaluating the fishery.

the seasonal anomalies, a tributary will not have more flow than the main stream it's flowing into. The study of lotic (flowing-water) habitats and lentic (standing-water) habitats is too vast to cover in this book. Suffice it to say that terms like "creek," "stream," "brook," and "river" are all just nebulous terms when it comes to determining how much water is flowing in them. But the more you know about this science, the better equipped you will be to research any fishery as to its aquatic insect life and trout species. With that in mind, there are some obvious clues without ever knowing the difference between first-order streams and second-order streams or erosion zones and depositional zones.

Perennial streams have continuous flows throughout the year as opposed to intermittent streams that do not. The map legend allows the fly fisher to easily distinguish between the two. As a general rule for the Montana high-country, streams that have no tributaries are not as productive as those that do and perennial streams are more productive than intermittent streams.

As explained earlier, every state in the United States has a website. For Montana I went to a site called "Government" looking for our Fish, Wildlife & Parks Department. Once there, I clicked on "Contact Us" and sent them an email asking who I might contact for fish-shocking data for the Blackfoot River drainage. A few days later I got an email from the biologist. I emailed him what I was looking for and he gave me the title of the report. I returned to the state library and checked out the report.

The information is out there, sometimes just a keystroke away. It may take some digging through the state government bureaus but when you find this pot of gold at the end of the rainbow, it's well worth it. There may be useful data hidden in places like university websites that have grants to study various aspects of fisheries. Forest Service websites can also provide data about recent burn areas, logging sites, or mining leases. What I also found was that the biologists really wanted people to read their reports. They worked very hard for that data and nothing makes them happier than someone else interested in the same things. They are out in the field, sometimes hand carrying large amounts of equipment long distances. When I've asked them for data, they have always quickly given it to me. But keep in mind that they are scientists, not politicians. They aren't going to make long-winded speeches about what a great job they are doing for the community. Instead of kissing babies, they study fish and their habitats. The data is there for you. You just have to let them know you want it. ∽

Camus Creek flows into the Flathead River in Glacier National Park.

CHAPTER THREE

Equipment and Gear

There are hundreds of fly-fishing gear manufacturers out there. Trying to sort through all the different models, lengths, and weights can be a daunting task. In the end it comes down to what tasks you want the gear to perform, how much annual usage it will receive, and then to some degree just how well it looks. Some gear tends to be long on looks and short on function.

Grandpa's old Ford Falcon was a reflection of him – no fancy tailfins or sequential taillights, just reliable as hell. He never pampered that car and I never remember it being clean. It smelled of dust, Old Gold cigarettes, Copenhagen, and dog. We'd finished hoeing the corn and were headed to the river to fish. It was hot and the backs of my bare legs were sticking to the vinyl seats. I swung my legs back and forth against the seat and it sounded like a giant band-aid each time I pulled them away from the sticky part. The windows were rolled down and the dust from the gravel road rolled into the car like fog on the deck of a ship. It swirled and landed on the dashboard, adding to the many previous layers that had come to make this car their home.

Normally we headed straight for the river, but this time we stopped in an old country store. Grandpa crushed out his cigarette in an overflowing ashtray and got out. I followed him up the thick wooden steps through the door that announced our entry with the sound of little silver bells.

Fly-fishing gear should be functional and never wear out. It should become an extension of your body and never be in the way. It should also have a certain panache.

" 'lo Carl." The man was on a ladder stocking shelves that were too high to reach for anyone but NBA players. His hello was genuine but muffled by the smoldering pipe that clicked in his teeth as he spoke.

"Morning," said grandpa.

They quickly got into a conversation about poor soil moisture and something that would kill gophers. I wandered off to explore the store and ended up at table full of tomatoes. But these were unlike any tomatoes I'd ever seen before; they were perfect. Standing on my tiptoes, I pulled one down and turned it over and

Good fly rods fit an angler's casting style. When the fly fisher ventures to different water, his style will change and so must his fly rod.

over in my hands. There were no worm marks. There were no hail marks. It was a perfect tomato!

"Grandpa, look at this tomato!" I eagerly offered it up to him like I'd just found the Holy Grail. "It's perfect!" I gushed.

"You don't want that son. It's a hot-house tomato," he answered, unimpressed by my miraculous find.

"Ah grandpa. I know you can't grow tomatoes in the house." This concept of indoor gardening wasn't something familiar to me and I took it as my grandpa pulling my leg.

"You don't want that tomato. It's no good." He sat down on a stool as he took the tomato from my hands.

"But it's perfect," I argued.

"Nah, it's a hot-house tomato. It's never seen a bird or worm or hail. It's like a lot of people you'll meet in your life – it looks good but it has nothing more going for it. Here, take a bite." He offered the perfect fruit to me for the final test. I took a bite expecting a taste to please the gods. Instead of delight, it had a dull taste, unlike any tomato I'd ever eaten.

"Yuck." I spit it into my hand and handed it to him. It was like eating a raw acorn.

Some fly-fishing equipment is a hot-house tomato.

Much of the fly-fishing gear sold today is meant to fit the needs of someone who will only fish a dozen or so days a year, and on varied sorts of water. It tends to fit the needs of all while not really fitting the needs of any. While small streams can be fly fished with a fast-action 6-weight, it would be like using a Mercedes to crack walnuts. In general, you want to think light and stealth.

Fly Rods

When it comes to fly rods, the word "light" can have a very different meaning to different people, but for most of the small streams of western Montana you'll want a light rod that will let you cast small dry flies accurately and delicately. It should also have enough backbone to allow you to turn a feisty cutthroat away from that pile of deadwood. A big thunderstick fly rod that

Small stream fly fishing puts different demands on equipment. Shorter casts and tighter quarters necessitates a dramatic gear change from big rivers.

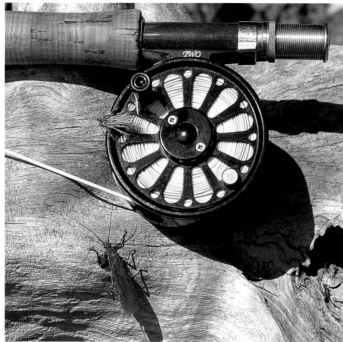

Matching a rod to a reel is critical, but equally crucial is balancing a fly line by considering the type and distance of your average cast.

All fly line manufacturers make various weight lines to match your rod and reel, but a closer look is necessary to match the line to your casting needs.

can cast your fly and line into the backing isn't very useful when 90 percent of your casts are less than 20 feet. You'll want a rod that allows you to feel the fish and to throw flies in the #14 to #20 range. There have been articles written about catching trout in small streams with weighted streamers, and while I'm sure these tactics work, I personally don't fish small streams to chuck heavily hackled AC Delco sparkplugs at small trout.

When choosing a fly rod for these streams, think 2-weight to 4-weight. Purchase a rod that's short enough to maneuver through willows, but keep in mind that there's a lot of roll casts in many situations and they work better with a bit more length. A rod with some backbone that is capable of making delicate deliveries is a plus. Weight-forward rather than double-taper lines are best because it's rare that you'll ever need to air out a line and cast more than twice the length of your car. My personal favorite, that fulfills all these needs, is a 2-weight 8.5-foot Sage XP. But fly rod preferences are about as varied as a flip-flop politician, so use what works best for you. A 5-weight or even 6-weight rod will work, but if you are going to purchase a new rod just for fishing small streams in western Montana, I would not go heavier than a 4-weight. I like a little longer rod for roll casting and dabbing and also for those streams that tend to be a bit more exposed to the wind. My backup rod is a 9-foot, 4-weight Sage SP.

Split cane and small stream fly fishing are the archetypal image of most fly fishers, but I have quite an aversion to pushing my way through thick willows with a delicate rod that long ago lost it's extra tip. I've seen plenty of rods broken by car doors, but I've also witnessed guys unsuccessfully try to spear a tree with a rod tip. With a bamboo rod in my hand I tend to shy away from certain areas just to protect the rod. Others don't share my fears.

Reels

Most of the time, reels for small stream fishing are simply used to tidy up the line at the end of the day. An expensive piece of lightweight aluminum carved to artistic perfection is likely overkill. Then one day you'll encounter that one fish that demands that ultra-smooth, stop-a-truck drag system, and that extra money you spent won't seem so lavish. Many of the small streams in western Montana are home to native bull trout. When one of these bad boys T-bones that 12-inch cutthroat on your line, you'll want to get a closer look at these inland barracudas. Playing these finned predators on a 2-weight puts the angler at a tremendous disadvantage. A good reel can sometimes save the day. Then there are those times when you encounter a small lake or large beaver pond where trout have a much larger area to run and here is where your gear will get tested. For this reason my reels of choice tend to be on the high end. For my 2-weight rod I use a Ross Vision One, and for my 4-weight I use an Abel 0.

Lines, Leaders, and Tippets

Matching your gear to a specific type of stream is crucial. What works really well in one situation may be a burden in another. The first consideration is the fly line itself and the physics of loading a rod. The standard gear here needs modification since most rods are designed to load best when the caster has more than 25 feet of line in the air plus the leader. For most small streams that is impractical. Over-weighting the rod by one or even two line weights will help solve the problem. Examine the fly line specifications closely. Most modern weight-forward lines have a 6- to 12-inch tip section before the front taper. If yours has more than 10 inches, cut it back. Very long tapers are not useful for short casts because it makes loading the rod difficult. Fly line manufacturers make lines for very specific uses but also offer general use lines. The trend seems to be lines that will cast longer distances, which are useless on small streams. At one time, Rio Products made a fly line designed specifically for small stream fly fishers. It was called Pocket Water, but it has been discontinued. Currently, the best line is the Rio Grand over-weighted one line weight. This line has a short front taper and is rated .5 over, thus one line weight over actually delivers 1.5 over, allowing it to load quickly with a minimal backcast. For my 2-weight rod I selected

a 3-weight Rio Grand line that results in an effective 3.5-weight line. The Rio Selective Trout line is a good second choice.

Using a shorter leader in heavily wooded areas where you have almost no room for a backcast will allow you to spend more time stalking trout and less time trying to retrieve your flies from trees and brush. I've encountered few situations outside of lakes and beaver ponds where I needed a leader longer than 7.5 feet. There are plenty of manufactured leaders available in both knotted and unknotted versions. Buy one that allows you to present the fly delicately with good turnover, but has enough tensile strength to stay intact if you happen to graze a leaf while casting.

Leaders start to fit into a very personalized area with fly fishers. Thirty or forty years ago every fishermen knew a series of

Balancing rod, reel, fly line, leader, and tippet will assure that you make better casts in tight situations.

When you find that perfect fishing spot where eager trout rise to your imitation, you should be fighting fish instead of your gear.

basic knots – it was simply part of the sport. Not knowing your knots would be like not knowing how to check the oil or tire pressure on your car. After four years in the Navy I learned knots that I will never use again in my life unless I end up buying a used battleship from salvage, but the skills of knot tying seem to have been lost with most of the Generation X and Y crowd. It's baffling to me how someone can write and troubleshoot lines of computer code but can't tie a blood knot. Let me cut to the chase – tie your own leaders. The braided, looped, and all the other techniques for leaders are mostly just to compensate for the fact that fly fishers either can't or don't want to learn to tie knots. No manufactured leader is going to cast or handle better than the one that you tie yourself and customize to a particular type of stream. The loop-to-loop system cannot cast better than one tied with a connecting knot and you will pay for your inability to tie knots with every single cast you make. I say this with a great deal of conviction because I've guided hundreds of fly fishers who showed up with loop systems. I would cut them off and replace them with a simple knot connector and every single one of them told me that their casting improved significantly.

Dry-fly leaders for small streams should be about two-thirds of the rod length to full rod length. I tie mine with stiffer butt sections using Maxima and the tippet sections with Rio PowerFlex. When you get into fussy fish on slow moving, glassy water, simply add a little bit of tippet, but trying to cast long leaders around piles of brush and wood debris is guaranteed to be frustrating. Cast the shortest leader you can get away with and finish it off with 4x or 5x tippet. If 4x tippet doesn't spook the fish it's best because it will make your presentations more accurate and allow you to better play the fish when it heads for the snags.

Fluorocarbon tippet materials are not great choices for dry fly fishermen. The specific gravity is greater than water, making it good for nymphs, but it tends to sink small dry flies. Tippet and leader materials vary between manufacturers. If you are curious, look up and compare the specifications of the top five and then compare diameter, tensile strength, shock strength, knot strength, and stiffness. It's a fascinating physics journey, but in

6' 5X KNOTTED LEADER

The formula for my favorite small-stream leader:

Use Maxima Chameleon for this butt section of the leader:

Diameter	Tippet size	Length
.017"	06X	18"
.015"	04X	14"
.012"	02X	6"

Use Rio PowerFlex for this tippet section of the leader:

Diameter	Tippet size	Length
.010"	1X	5"
.008"	3X	4"
.007"	4X	4"
.006"	5X	21"

the end you'll likely end up using what works best for your particular style and brand loyalty. Rio PowerFlex tippet is my choice. Keep in mind that all brands are susceptible to both heat and UV light. Store your spare tippet in a cool, dark place. I have found that a few feet of tippet, or even an entire spool, are cheaper than a couple of flies. Replace your tippet material if you have any suspicion that the failure rate is too high.

My best recommendation is to throw away your leader straighteners. They generate too much heat, which in turn fatigues the leader. You won't feel the heat because that piece of leather won't allow it to reach your fingers. Instead, to straighten a leader slowly pull it through your bare hands with enough speed and tension to create some heat. When the heat feels like it's about to burn your hand, stop. This will enable you to keep the heat level low and it also will help you find problem areas. Inspect your leaders and tippet for abrasions, wind knots, or weak spots.

Clothing and Layering

What we buy and wear outdoors is very important and often overlooked. Some of the most productive fly fishing is done when the weather has driven the unprepared into the safety of their vehicles and rendered them miserable. Fortunately, the science of outdoor clothing arrived to solve this problem.

My clothing is mostly Patagonia, including my fishing vest. Patagonia is simply the best clothing out there and if you have a problem, they are quick to solve or replace the item. In the long run their gear will save you money. Most of us have heard that

A good rule of thumb is that the tougher the stream is to access, the less likely it will be that the fish have seen many anglers.

dressing in layers is a good idea. Few people seem to actually know what that really means. Simply put, you want to stay warm and dry when it is cold and wet.

There are a few ways to get wet. It can come from the elements or it can come from your own body via heat, perspiration, or condensation. Moisture will move heat away from your body, so the next-to-the-skin layer is designed to wick moisture away. The type of material is critical. Too much or the wrong type of clothing and you'll sweat, too little and your body temperature will drop. Not all layers are created alike. Cotton is comfortable and cool, but it retains moisture. If you wear cotton underwear it will absorb the moisture from your body and the humidity in the air and keep it close to your skin, giving you a cold, clammy sensation. It can also lead to a drop in your core body temperature known as hypothermia. There are lots of better choices. Patagonia makes underwear shorts and T-shirts from Capilene and other synthetics. This material moves moisture away from your body and hands it off to the next layer until it's away from your skin. Next is an insulating layer if the temperature or conditions warrant. This layer or layers, often made of fleece, puts a barrier between you and the cold that allows you to retain heat. The final is the outer layer to protect from the elements. GoreTex is used mostly for this function. It's light, comfortable, and magically keeps moisture out while allowing reasonable amounts of condensation to escape. It also functions as a windbreak. Fleece is a wonderful material, but by itself it doesn't stop the wind.

The best gear will always remain a matter of personal taste and experience. If you ask a salesperson, the answer will likely be something he has in stock. Personally, I'm always searching for that better mousetrap, comparing it to gear I've used for years that has served me well. Much of the new and improved is merely new.

A small landfill wouldn't hold the pile of outdoor gear I've worn out, broken, or discarded. In my world, gear should do its job each and every time I use it and never fail. It should never spook fish and never be in my way. Clothing should move with me and become a comfortable second skin, simultaneously protecting me from the elements. It should also have certain panache without being ostentatious. Rods should be well balanced, fit my hand, and respond to my casting style for the given water. Then there are the simple things like fly boxes that should open and close easily so I don't end up launching the contents into the ionosphere. Each of us has hundreds of personal likes and dislikes when it comes to gear, and we make purchasing decisions based on those needs.

The simple answer is to be prepared but don't carry more than you'll need. In a quickly changing mountain environment that means layers and a good raincoat. I've guided fly fishers for many years. I've yet to see anyone standing in a rain or snowstorm, soaked to the skin, and brag about how much money they saved by buying cheap rain gear. There are great bargains out there and everyone should work within a budget. If you are going into the high country, know that it can snow any month of the year. If you are dry, you'll have a great story to tell your friends. If you are wet long enough that your body's core temperature drops to dangerous levels, you might not be telling them a happy story. Hypothermia is the lowering of your body temperature. Because we fly fishers are in and around water, the chances of us getting wet are great. Fight hypothermia with your head – go prepared and dress in layers with no cotton.

What to put all the gear you carry in can sometimes be the most important decision you make all day. Some vests have abundant pockets just begging for things to fill them, but few vests have adjustable shoulder straps, so a small day pack can often be just the answer. Day packs are a must for certain streams where a long walk may be necessary. If you wear a shirt with large pockets, often your essential flies can go in your shirt along with the requisite nippers, extra tippet and other "have to have" gear.

Advertisers want us to buy their products.

They sell us on the notion that if we are to attract a member of the opposite sex we need to smell good, look good, and appear as if we would be a good provider. Fish are only concerned about whether we might kill them. They hide in those logjams because it protects them from predators like us. They won't come out to see your shiny Rolex or to smell your Italian cologne. The opposite is true. If the flash of your watch or jewelry happens to reflect to their part of the stream, they will retreat to their safety zone. They can't detect the odor of your cologne in the air like grizzly bears, but they can detect almost anything on a fly just as it's almost in their mouths.

While purchasing a vest, choosing the right size and style will ensure that you carry just what you need for that day and nothing more.

Trout "taste" much like a toddler and are quick to expel anything that is foreign. Studies show that they have a strong aversion for anything based on petroleum or alcohol and an affinity for dairy. Use this information to your advantage. Forgo the aftershave, cologne, and deodorant. The chance of offending another fly fisher in Montana's high country with your natural body odor is pretty minute. Leave the jewelry at home or in your pocket. If you fill your gas tank that morning, or put on sunscreen, wash your hands with a non-deodorant soap. Lemon or limejuice will neutralize just about any smell, but it's acidic. Bow hunters have this smell stuff down to a science. A trip to a sporting goods store or bow hunter website will give you lots of tips to reducing your scent, but as fly fishers you only have to deal with what will go on the fly in order to catch fish. However you achieve it, in general, just try to make your flies odorless and your appearance reflection free.

about as flexible as a frozen garden hose, and offered zero insulation in either heat or cold.

I fish with the intensity of a mountain lion waiting for that mule deer fawn to stray just a little farther from the doe. Consequently I end up stepping in up-to-the-logo holes in rivers and streams while watching a fish rise methodically to dry flies. I'm totally mesmerized by rising fish and see no reason to change even if I thought I could. Sneaking up on a rising fish in close quarters must trigger some very primitive part of my brain when men used to stalk prey with sharp sticks so they could feed the rest of the clan while being hailed as some sort of hunter savior. While the thought of sitting half naked around a camp fire with parasite infested, toothless clan members doesn't hold a lot of appeal to me, the stalking of trout makes me feel more alive than just about any other human activity.

Waders

When I was a young high school kid fishing the small streams of the Colorado high country I stayed away from waders and fished exclusively with hip boots. These were the days before neoprene and the waders at the time were heavy rubber designed to keep you dry and comfortable as long as you never left the tailgate of your truck where you put them on in the first place. After making three or four steps toward the river, you were miserable because they were heavy,

Breathable waders are a quantum leap in fly fishing. The angler can now be truly comfortable under a wide variety of weather and water conditions.

As a result, I like to wear waders because then I can move through the stream with ease and not worry about filling my hip boots with water. I've tried several different brands of GoreTex waders and they get better every year. The Simms and the Patagonia brands work best for me. I'm currently using Patagonia because they offer an easy waist-high option. When the temperatures rise during the Montana summers, it's nice to have some air moving around my upper torso. They also pack well into the back pocket of my vest, allowing me to hike

Waders should be tough enough to handle the rigors of wood debris, logs, and snags while keeping you dry and warm when wading the deep holes.

out of an area with just my wading boots and lightweight pants. Even the best waders will not move 100 percent of the sweat and condensation away from your skin if you're on a fast-paced sprint on a backcountry road or trail in 90-degree heat. I also like the Patagonia wading boots because they offer great support while hiking on rough trails and they are lightweight. I tend to unintentionally kick rocks with my toes and these boots hold up to my abuse.

Eye Protection

A good pair of polarized sunglasses is a must to see into those pools and to protect your eyes from the intense UV light of high elevations. While walking through thick trees or heavy brush,

Fly fishing can be a gadget-oriented sport, but some tools, like hemostats, when used properly, will greatly reduce fish mortality.

sunglasses also protect your eyes from abrasion. Westslope cutthroats are native Montana fish and have adapted well to the environment. They are very well camouflaged and tough to see even with ideal conditions, which makes good polarized glasses a necessity rather than an option.

Hydration

Carrying water may often be inconvenient. Dehydration is worse. One choice is to carry water; another is to buy and carry one of the many water filtration systems available. Some systems look like a regular water bottle but have the filter built into it. These are great options in that you can keep drinking water all day long without having the bulk or weight of bottled water. A cooler full of iced down beer in your car can be a great reward at the end of the day, but keep in mind that beer won't rehydrate you. If the weather is very hot and dry, a product like Gatorade makes more sense to prevent muscle cramps associated with the loss of electrolytes.

Miscellaneous Gear

Floatant is necessary to dress dry flies. I have used many different brands and types and found that silicon-based liquid works best when the fly is completely dry, but using too much is counterproductive. Hold the fly and then squirt a small amount on your thumbnail. Lightly paint the fly with even smaller amounts by dabbing and then applying it only to the parts you want to float, like the wing or hackle. When dressing parachute patterns, do not dress the abdomen since you want it to sit low in the surface film. After you've used the fly and it's wet, again hold the fly in your fingers, blow off the excess water, and then apply a dry, desiccant powder. These drying agents have been around for a number of years. Originally they came in a canister with a snapping lid. Snapping the lid shut to shake the fly inside will bruise and decrease the strength of the tippet. Newer products have a brush inside the bottle that works really well but they tend to be on the pricey side. I reuse their bottles by filling them with a product called Fletch Dry that can be purchased from archery supply stores. It's used for drying feathers on arrows, works really well, and offers a substantial savings. Know that all these products are drying agents and if you transfer the powder from your finger to your eye, it won't be an experience you'll want to repeat anytime soon.

Hemostat-type tools are a must for crimping barbs and split shot, and they return to their design roots for hook removal. Some of these can also double as a catch-and-release tool by sliding them over the tippet to extract the fly from the fish.

For those with failing close-up eyesight, some sort of magnification is a must, especially in low light situations. A few years ago I discovered a wonderful product called a Surefire flashlight. This tiny marvel puts out an incredible amount of light and can attach to the bill of a baseball cap, leaving your hands free for tying on the caddis pattern just before dark. It could also double for a headlight on your car.

Many fly fishers leave their net at home when fishing a small stream. I have often found that on fast moving water, a good net can capture the fish much more efficiently than chasing the fish by hand and better hold it while you remove the hook. Rubber mesh models reduce the friction between the fish and the net and do the least amount of harm to the trout. Knotted nylon collapses on the gills and tangles both the fish and the dropper fly.

One of the most important tools in your vest will always be a thermometer; one with a decent metal covering to protect it from breaking is a must. A small lanyard will allow you to suspend it in the water instead of using a numb hand. Trout die off in water temperatures over 75 degrees because there is too little oxygen and

too much bacteria. When water temperatures are below mid-30s, their metabolism slows to the point where they feed very little. The ideal temperatures are from the mid-50s to the mid-60s, with temperatures above 50 degrees showing signs of significant activity.

Many fly fishers don't carry a thermometer because they don't understand how essential water temperatures are to hatching insects. Even a cursory knowledge is rewarded.

CHAPTER FOUR

The Fish Hunt

Catching wild, native westslope cutthroat in fast moving mountain streams comes with the challenge of keeping them out of the piles of logs and sunken sticks they seem to love. These cutts are seldom found very far from the cover of undercut banks or dead brush unless there's a major source of food, and even then they are reluctant to venture far from the shelters. One tactic many of us have used when fishing a new stream is to intentionally walk through likely holding areas and then look for fish darting out in all directions. This seldom works for these native cutthroats. More often than not they will remain far back under the woodpiles and if you walk through a hole near them, they simply retreat further. You'll rarely ever see them spook like a rainbow or brown. Many a fly fisher will conclude that there are no fish in a stream because they used this technique and it didn't work.

Westslope cutthroat have evolved over the years to perfectly match the river's substrate. When they are motionless and not actively looking for food, they are difficult to spot. Unless the light is just right, you'll seldom see them even when they are out in the open searching for food. Then the magic happens and suddenly there are fish flashing for nymphs or taking natural adult dry flies from the surface. They seem to appear out of nowhere. One minute you're convinced the stream is sterile and void of fish, and the next minute

The author ponders fly selection while fishing in grizzly-bear country in Glacier National Park. He carries Counter Assault bear spray and a water filtration system on his wading belt.

there seem to be fish everywhere actively feeding. The science behind the magic is water temperature, which governs insect activity. When the magic begins, be ready.

Few of us fly fishers have the discipline to arrive at any stream and then just sit and observe. We want to get in there and start casting as soon as possible even if observation is a better choice. Many clues about a fishery may be obvious in the form of wildlife. The presence of osprey, eagles, cranes, herons, or kingfishers is a clear indication there are fish around. Dippers are a sign that the substrate has aquatic insects. But even if you see none of these indicators, there may still be plenty of fly-fishing opportunities and the first tool out of your vehicle should be a seine.

If you can't resist the temptation to hit the stream, at least pull out that thermometer while you're casting and take the water temperature. If the temperature is in the 50s, that's a good sign.

Bull trout are protected and must be returned to the water immediately. This photo was taken with special permission from Montana Fish, Wildlife & Parks.

Below 50 degrees and the dry fly action will generally be non-existent. Few streams in the high country of western Montana ever get above 60 degrees unless there's a major forest fire on both sides of the stream.

In most small streams, the areas where the fish will most likely be holding are obvious once you've caught several fish in those areas, sometimes not so obvious before you do.

Beaver Ponds

These are easy to spot and even easier to fish. Not all beaver ponds hold fish. Look for ponds that have a substantial amount of water discharging out the downstream end. Most retain the stream channel and that is usually the deepest part of the pond. The best approach is from the downstream side. The fish will mostly face up current and this stealth approach comes in from their blind side. It also normally allows you a decent corridor for a backcast over the stream. Trout in beaver ponds are often a bit larger and require a delicate presentation on the slower moving water. Take the time to lengthen your leader and if needed go down a tippet size. The first cast in any pond is the most important. Sometimes the first fish is the only one you'll get, especially if you hook the Alpha trout and he runs all over the pond scaring the hell out all the juveniles. Cast short first and then cast your way further into the pond on successive tries. Use as little fly line as possible and watch the line you are stripping at your feet to make sure it doesn't tangle around the wooden debris of the dam. A better technique is to strip your fly line in loops around your hand.

Trout Behavior

Toddlers quickly learn the physics of cause and effect. They push the doorbell button and the effect is a noise. It's great fun for them and they can do it for hours on end despite the scolding from mom or dad. They later begin to learn more complex and abstract thought; if you plug a lamp into an outlet, turning the

Knowing where to cast is just as important as knowing how. Rick and Jill Oie fish together on Copper Creek.

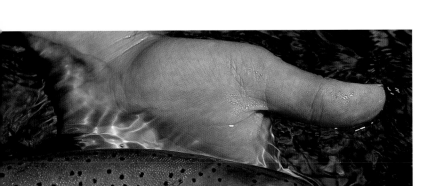

Westslope cutthroats are native Montana trout. They are beautiful, fiesty, and fragile creatures.

While rainbow trout are not native to most Rocky Mountain streams, all those in Montana are wild and haven't been stocked in moving waters since 1973.

switch on the lamp makes the light come on. They quickly see these sorts of secondary relationships. Confusion comes in when they figure out how to pry that childproof safety cap off the outlet and put, say, a bobby pin in the wall outlet. What lights up is their little hand and arm. My son did this, but only once.

After I began guiding in Montana, I quickly realized that most experienced fly fishers were taking what they learned on other rivers and demanding that it work on new ones. Where the hatchery rainbows were holding on a slow moving chalk creek in Pennsylvania with water temps in the high 60s weren't where the westslope cutthroats were holding in a fast moving backcountry stream with temperatures in the 40s.

As fly fishers, we tend to lock in our thoughts regarding what has worked in the past. When the fishery is different and the methods that served a fly fisher well elsewhere are failing, the successful fly fisher adapts. If you find yourself casting over and over with zero results, step back for a moment to analyze the problem.

Reading water presents quite a challenge to the beginner, but a few simple explanations should help even the more experienced fly fisher. Trout need food, oxygen, and shelter from predators. Despite what intelligence you might attribute to these creatures, they are little more than a brain stem with fins. They primarily use sight, but secondarily taste, to distinguish their food from all the other detritus and debris in the drift. Trout cannot survive in the long term by expending more calories than they ingest, so it comes down to stimulus/response. If a fly fisher spooks a fish (stimulus) the trout swims away (response). If the fly fisher drifts an artificial fly that resembles what the fish is currently eating (stimulus), the fish will take the fly into its mouth (response).

Shelter from predators and safe haven from the fast moving current is a primary instinct for trout. If an angler, heron, or raccoon is pursuing a fish, the fish isn't concerned about food, so the first place to look for trout is one where there is refuge of some kind. It might be an undercut bank, a logjam, or simply deeper water that makes seeing them difficult. The same places are also where the current is slowed by the structure, making feeding easier. If there are enough insects, the fish will sometimes abandon their primary shelter in order to gorge. In a normal situation though, they will hold in areas close to, but not in, the current line. This conveyor belt delivers food and oxygen, but in cold-water situations trout will generally not expend the extra calories needed to fight the current while they wait for food. The structure of the stream acts as a barrier to the current's velocity. Water moves slower just downstream of structure, and sometimes, in an eddy situation, it actually moves upstream. These areas allow fish to spot insects that are being transported by the current while holding in water adjacent to the current, thus expending a minimal amount of energy.

The Stealth Approach

Small streams are not well manicured or even have many paths along their banks like the well-traveled and close-to-town fisheries. Often you'll find them choked with foliage and deadwood piles, making navigation and stealth a bit of a challenge. I normally like to fish upstream because it allows me the opportunity to see the fish before they see me, as most often they are looking upstream or more correctly up current, because that is where the food comes from.

I will use anything available to hide my profile. I'll stand behind or next to large boulders or foliage to break my 6-foot, 3-inch profile. A crouching or kneeling stance also works well in many cases. In many streams where I know I'll spend a great part of the day kneeling, I wear a pair of construction kneepads to protect my waders as well as my patella.

Often just shade will make you nearly invisible to the fish. While I haven't gone so far as to wear camouflage clothing, I try to wear colors often found in nature, avoiding white and yellow because it spooks fish. Jewelry is shiny and reflects sunlight. There are guys out there writing about hitting their graphite rods with steel wool to take the shine off. Gary LaFontaine was the king of stealth and came up with a stealth rod that has a dull finish. Every little bit helps. A slow approach is always better than

crashing into a hole and then expecting the fish to do anything but head for cover. The key is to not let the fish know you are there.

Riseforms and Presentation

Few novice or even intermediate dry fly anglers understand trout behavior and how trout routinely feed because they mostly fixate on their fly and their casting instead of taking a moment to observe the fish itself.

The area of the stream that a trout can see as it searches for

Trout will generally face upstream when a hatch occurs. One easy method to conceal your presence is to cast upstream with a delicate presentation.

food is referred to as a window. The size of that window depends on several factors, including the clarity of water, structure, and the depth of the water. The clarity is determined by the percentage of dirt or detritus that is in the water. Structure such as wood debris or boulders may block the trout's view of the surface. The depth of the water where trout are holding is a huge factor. The deeper the water the larger visual angle they have to the surface, but clarity and structure may negate this advantage. Also, if the

Trout in very cold, high-country streams do not occupy the same holding spots as their lower elevation cousins. They prefer the ease of water slowed by structure.

water is too deep and too fast for the fish to hold near the surface, the trout will continue to feed on subsurface fare that is closer and more efficient to obtain. The following paragraphs refer to the illustrations on pages 56 and 57.

(Illustration One). The fish is holding in slower current that is blocked by structure. When the hatch begins and insects appear in the drift with enough frequency, the trout will often move into position near the feeding lanes or at least position itself for a good view of the surface. Depending on the intensity of the hatch and the water temperature, fish find the most energy-efficient positions. Larger trout will dominate the most advantageous positions, pushing smaller trout away.

(Illustration Two). The fish identifies the fly as food. When the fly floats into the trout's vision window, the trout begins its ascent to the surface. Now, away from the refuge of its holding spot, the trout raises its head toward the surface and is pushed downstream by the same current the fly is riding. This method allows the trout to use minimal swimming effort to pursue the fly as the current does most of the work, with the trout making minor adjustments with its tail and fins in order to match the travel of the fly. The trout uses the current and its body to move into position to take the fly. Often the fly will lift off the surface of water before the trout reaches it, so energy conservation by the fish is very important.

(Illustration Three). Many times, particularly in slower moving water, the trout will hang just below the fly and watch it for a moment before either taking the fly or refusing it. It's looking for a primary and sometimes a secondary trigger. That trigger will likely be either size or silhouette. It's rarely ever color on dry flies because trout are looking into the light and are likely just seeing subdued colors. The first thing to try if you see this behavior and are getting refusals is to get a better drift. If the fly is leaving a wake because of drag, few fish will fall for this obvious fraud. Reducing your tippet size is next. Tippet can affect the fly's drift if it makes the fly look too stiff or unnatural. However, it's rarely the tippet size itself (within reason) on these quick moving freestone streams. Next, try clipping the hackle from the belly side of your fly, check to make sure the hair wing hasn't spun around to the bottom side of the hook shank. Then check the tail and bend it upwards if needed. What you can do on the stream to a pattern will depend largely on how the artificial was tied, the style, and too many other factors to name, but generally speaking, look closely at the fly and modify it so that it will ride lower in the water. That may mean pulling off hackle or even dubbing, it may mean clipping away some of the wing or trimming a collar on the fly. If all this fails, change the fly. If you look around and the air is filled with caddis and you have a mayfly pattern tied on, the problem is obvious. That's rarely the case. When the pattern is the culprit it's almost always size or style. As humans, we think that if the fish isn't interested in a 16-ounce T-bone, we'll offer him a 22-ouncer. Switching to a smaller size is opposite of what we're inclined to do, but it's almost always better to go smaller than larger. Fish don't think because they have no real brain. We humans tend to put our thoughts into the mind of a fish, but the fish has no mind either, so bigger fails and smaller succeeds in almost every case.

(Illustration Four). The take, or more accurately, the suck. The trout breaches and takes the fly from the surface by opening its mouth under the fly and expelling water out its gills. This pulls the fly into the fish's mouth. As the trout quickly closes its mouth to prevent escape, you will sometimes see a bubble form on the surface in the riseform ring. The riseform rings, along with the fish, are still moving downstream in the current. The second aspect to study is that the riseform rings take a moment to expand to a size large enough for us to see.

(Illustration Five). This trout turns away from the faster water of the current and toward the slower moving and often upstream current of an eddy. It turns its body to decrease drag.

(Illustration Six). Return. This trout rides the upstream eddy current for an energy-free ride back to its original holding spot to look for the next prey.

Looking at this series of illustrations, it's clear that if you cast

Westslope cutthroats will often rise to a well tied dry fly and then, after feeling the hook, take the angler on a lively ride through piles of wood debris.

to the riseform or, worse yet, downstream of the riseform, the fish won't even know the fly is there. If you put the fly exactly where the fish first saw it in its window, it's a good presentation only if the delivery is perfect. If you slap the fly on the water, drag it through the window, or slap, drag, and recast, the fish is on notice that something is very wrong. At this point it's looking for heron legs or the splash and plunge of an osprey or eagle. The safe solution is to cast a bit further upstream and allow your fly to drift easily into the fish's window. All of this depends on your casting accuracy, presentation, and the particular stream situation. Casting too far upstream may cause your fly to drag by the time it reaches the trout's window or there may be structure in the way.

Knowledge is only part of the equation. If you show up at the stream and can't cast accurately, all the knowledge in the world won't put fish on your fly. Often times you will be required to land a fly on a target with only an inch or two margin for error. Too far one way and the fly lands in the brush, too far the other way and it's out of the feeding lane. Casting practice can be done in your backyard, city park, or even in a parking lot. Traveling hundreds or thousands of miles to practice casting is often done, but it is never efficient.

Illustration One – Visual Contact

As the current hits the rock just upstream of this trout, it is slowed, creating a mini-eddy just downstream of the rock. The trout will wait in this slower water because it requires less energy. The trout will move into these areas when a hatch begins because aquatic insects are concentrated along current lanes, like the one where the current is squeezed between the two rocks. As the insects struggle to emerge from their nymphal or pupal stages, they are vulnerable to predation. If there are several fish present, the larger ones will dominate, often running the smaller fish out or away from the prime feeding areas. Sometimes a smaller fish will dart in and steal a fly before the larger fish can take it.

Illustration Two – Pursuit

The trout identifies the insect as possible food and begins its pursuit, using the current as it moves out of the shelter of the rock. Approaching the fly, the trout raises its head for a closer inspection. This move also exposes more of the fish's body to the push of the current, allowing it to match the speed of the prey with minimal energy. The trout need only make minor adjustments as it nears the fly.

If the insect lifts off the surface, the fish will drop its head and return to its original holding spot.

Illustration Three – Identification

The trout hangs just below the fly, looking for an identification trigger, while matching the insect's speed as both move downstream in harmony. If the trout finds that particular stimulus, it will take the fly; if not, it will refuse it. Refusals are the subject of countless magazine articles. Making on-stream corrections are necessary to get the fish to accept your fly.

Illustration Four – The Take

The physics of the take are complex. Since trout don't have the means to place the fly into their mouths, they instead move very close to the fly and then suck it in by expelling water out their gills. This creates a vacuum that pulls the insect into the trout's open mouth. To prevent the fly from escaping, the fish will normally quickly close its mouth, often leaving an air bubble on the surface.

The riseform rings begin to expand and move downstream with the fish.

Illustration Five – The Turn

After the fish takes the fly, it will turn its head down and begin to move out of the current and away from the surface. The riseform rings continue to expand and move downstream.

Illustration Six – The Return

The trout moves away from the pull of the current and begins its return journey back to its original holding spot. Many times the fish will move into an eddy current that is moving back upstream. This provides the fish with a current to ride and minimizes expended energy.

Runs, Pools, Riffles, and Pocket Water

Structure, gradient, or both form a riffle. This small stretch of miniature white water oxygenates the water and in some cases provides cover for the trout. It's very important to the fish. Riffles are visual cues to most anglers who normally frequent warmer waters. The faster water is cooler than the eddies. But for fish in most of the Montana high country, they aren't looking to cool off;

just the opposite; they are mostly looking to warm up. So for the most part, these riffles that served you so well on other streams are not going to be productive if you are looking for top-water action.

The runs in any stream are where the water slows but where most of the food items, free in the drift, are found. These are prime feeding areas, especially if there is structure present. If there is no structure, the trout will likely move to these areas to feed but when the hatch is over, they retreat to safer habitat. Often, here is where you will find the foam lines. This gives you a visual reference to where the food items are concentrated. Foam can also create a fluid cover for the fish, giving them a sense of security while they actively feed. These runs, particularly on colder streams, are almost always the most productive fishing spots.

Pools can be formed by a variety of structures or just because the river is deeper. In many mountain streams you can observe fish holding on the bottom of these surprisingly deep pools. It is where I've often observed bull trout. If you spend enough time on Montana's western-slope, high-country streams, you will likely see a bull trout chase, and sometimes eat, a fish you have hooked. It's an amazing event of nature and one you'll relive over and over in your mind. I've unintentionally hooked and released bull trout in the eight- to nine-pound range and have seen photos of some that are twice that size. These highly predacious members of the char family seem to have an affinity for these deep areas of streams.

Pools can be productive but often drag-free presentations are tough because of the different currents. Your fly is drifting one direction and your fly line is moving in

The best places to find rising trout in high-country streams are those areas where water can warm easily.

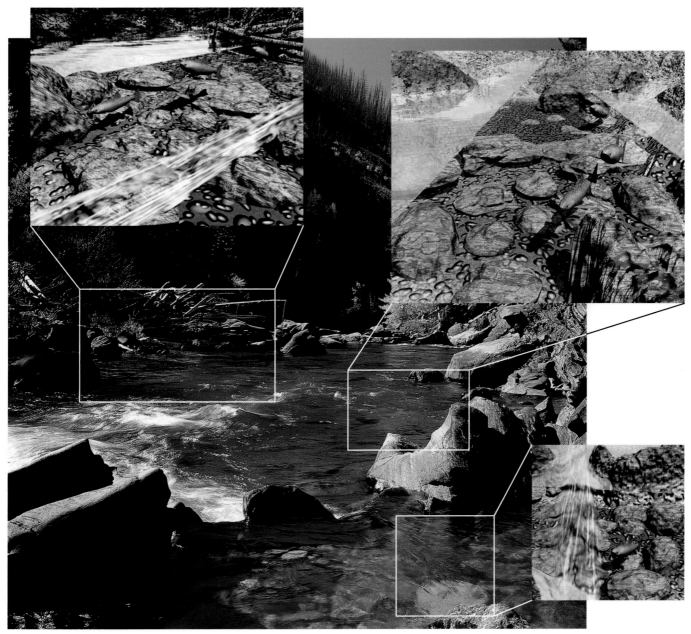

Top left – Trout will hold in the eddy formed by the large rock on the left. This allows them a clear view of what the current is drifting down to them. Also note the fish hiding under the wood pile. Middle right – Again the fish are holding in the slower water just downstream from the large rock. Bottom right – While there isn't room for many fish, these small pockets often are home to one or two trout. Here the water is slowed as it bounces off the large rock just downstream. Note the absence of fish in the very fast moving water of mid-stream. Fish will only move into these areas if the water temperatures rise above 60°F.

another. In many smaller eddy pools, the best tactic is to dab the fly from a hidden position. This involves holding all the fly line and most of your tippet off the water. Move the tip of your rod along and match the speed of the current with the fly. It involves a lot of stealth, but catching a fish at this close range is very exciting. Before you dab the fly for the first time, figure out where you

Differing water conditions and environments necessitate adaptation on the part of the angler.

could land the fish without pulling it onto the bank or wood debris. It's a challenge but well worth the effort.

Pocket water is a little oasis for trout. It's where the water velocity, usually among rapids, comes to a halt or even moves upstream in the eddy. These are areas of great turbulence with small pockets of quiet. It's also usually the most dangerous part of a trout stream to wade so great caution is needed. For this reason these areas usually are fished very little.

Trout expend little energy to hold in these pockets while their food is stranded here during hatches. Many pockets are so small that oftentimes only one or two fish will take up residence. Casting into these pockets doesn't usually work because the water is moving very quickly, and many are better suited to high-stick techniques using nymphs or dabbing with dry flies.

High stick is accomplished when you slowly move toward the target, being careful not to spook the fish. Then, keeping your fly line off the water to prevent drag, you simply drift the often-weighted nymph through the fish while keeping the rod tip high. The fish are right under your rod tip and you'll feel the takes. This prevents drag but requires some real stealth to get within a rod's length of the fish.

Dabbing imitates the movements of aquatic insects as they lay eggs on the water in an up and down motion, which is often followed by a short drift as the eggs are deposited. It's this egg-laying behavior that dabbing imitates. With the same stealth techniques as high sticking, approach the fish and then in a 'yo-yo' motion bounce the fly onto the surface for a second and then lift. If the conditions permit, allow the fly a short downstream drift before picking up. Most people I've taught this method have thought I was taking them on the proverbial snipe hunt until suddenly a trout comes up and takes their fly. It's a lot of fun but requires patience when moving to the target. I like to use a large log or rock to hide behind if possible and to approach from downstream. When I was younger I would put a split shot above my dry fly to keep it from swinging in the wind and moving it off target. I used a 10-foot fiberglass rod to keep me further away and would often lie on my belly on banks to get close enough. This sort of stealth pays great dividends on the stream, and while I still use many of the techniques of my boyhood, I'm seldom willing to crawl very far for a fish.

Spotting Trout

When trout are actively feeding on a smooth surface it's usually pretty obvious, but if they are rising in shade, foam, broken water, or while it's raining, you may not notice the rises without careful observation. Generally speaking, spotting rising trout is not difficult on small streams after a little practice. The most common mistake fly fishers make is to look for a large splashy rise instead of a very subtle one. If you are looking for a very subtle take, the big splashy rises won't go unnoticed. The reverse is not true.

I rely heavily on polarized sunglasses to cut the surface glare. They make wade fishing much safer and it is nearly impossible to see fish on the bottom without them. But vision alone is not the answer. Knowing where to look for rising fish is usually a more important factor. Given all this, there is one small stream axiom to remember – fish will sometimes rise to a dry fly when you haven't seen a rise all day. Actively rising fish on these sorts of streams is a luxury but certainly not a prerequisite. The amount of edible biomass in these waters is a fraction of what you will find in a tailwater, so waiting until the fish are in a frenzy feeding mode will only happen a few times each summer. Prospecting your fly in "fishy water" is the answer.

When trout, especially cutthroat trout, venture out of their hiding spots to feed on an active hatch, they normally begin feeding on the nymphs or emergent pupae first. Careful observation will reveal flashes as they turn their body to capture vulnerable prey. The best tactic during this phase is a dry fly with a beadhead dropper. My favorites are a Beadhead Peacock

Soft Hackle for caddis or a Beadhead Lovebug for mayflies. Then, when the trout begin to shift their focus to the surface, you can easily clip off the dropper and fish the single dry fly. Matching the hatch at this point will depend heavily on your knowledge and experience of aquatic entomology. While small streams are not nearly as technical as spring creeks or heavily fished tailwaters, the less time you spend guessing and employing trial and error methods, the more time you'll have to actually catch fish.

Trout can be very difficult to spot without polarized sunglasses, while some stand out more.

On the North Fork of the Blackfoot the structure is often large boulders. These provide great pools where the water slows and warms.

Analyze the Substrate

I find myself quite fascinated by aquatic insects. Yes, I'm aware that people who collect and study bugs are considered giant dorks by most. I thought that also until I began my exploratory journey into this very ancient underwater world of aquatic entomology. These tiny creatures go through an amazing metamorphosis. They begin life as a very tiny egg on the bottom of the stream, clinging to whatever home the current finds for them. Then, extracting oxygen from the water, they eat and grow to insect adolescence. For some, this period of their life is as long as five years; for others it's as short as several weeks. Some have legs and crawl, some are flat and cling to the substrate, some burrow, and many others build their own shelters as well as a spider-like, underwater web to catch their food. All are susceptible to predators such as dippers and of course fish. They can be stranded when water levels drop or swept away by irrigation pumps into a rancher's pasture. Finally their day of maturity arrives and they go from breathing underwater to suddenly flying and breathing air. As they float on the surface trying to dry their wings, there's always that threat from the fish and their instinct tells them to hurry to take to the air, where they discover a whole new set of predators such as swallows. Through sheer mass of numbers some live to reproduce, lay eggs, and continue a cycle that has gone largely unchanged for hundreds of millions of years.

Aquatic insects are amazing creatures. With very few exceptions, they don't bite or sting. They can be tough to get off your windshield when they mistakenly identify the highway as a stream, but then I've seen human teenagers who think the street is a skateboard park. If you have the time to explore this amazing world of aquatic entomology, I think you'll find the journey quite rewarding. Plus, when you walk to a stream and see insects, you'll be much more adept at choosing which fly to tie on your tippet and how to fish it.

Normally you will find yourself on a high-country stream in western Montana way too early to see fish rising. Until the water temperature reaches the low to mid 50s, there isn't much activity. This is a good time to check out the substrate. Since the streams covered in this book deal mostly with western Montana watersheds, the following information pertains to that region. The recipes for these patterns can be found in Chapter 10.

An accurate thermometer is a very important tool and the magic water temperature is right around 50 degrees Fahrenheit.

There are no absolutes in fly fishing. Here, on the warmer stretches of Rock Creek, Rick Oie finds plenty of eager brown trout in the faster riffles.

The October Caddis begin showing up on most Montana streams in late September. Their large size catches the attention of the trout.

This October Caddis is ready to pupate and will retreat into its stone and stick case when alarmed. This one measured nearly an inch in length.

Below 45 degrees there isn't much insect activity and the fish, especially westslope cutthroat trout, tend to stay well out of sight in the safety of brush and wood. As the temperature nears 50 degrees, the nymphs that are near maturity prepare to move to the surface for their grand finale. When this happens, particularly when the migration to the surface begins, the fish move from their hiding spots and you'll see flashes as they take nymphs both from the bottom and from between the bottom and the surface. At this time, by just holding a seine in the current, you will know what's in the drift. But usually when the fish are actively feeding, you're not going to walk back to your vehicle to grab a seine. A better tactic is to do this task early when the fishing is slow.

There are many commercial seines available, and most of them will work well. I carry two different seines. One stays mostly in my truck or raft as it's large. It works great but wouldn't be practical to carry on the stream as you fish. It's easy to make. Using two 4-feet x 1-inch dowels, either staple or screw a piece of 5-foot x 3-foot window screen to each of the dowels. Center the 3-foot screen on the 4-foot dowels so that you have 6 inches on the top of the dowels for handholds and 6 inches on the bottom to dig with. The second seine I carry is a pair of white women's panty hose with the legs knotted and cut off. This slips over my stream net and is carried easily in my vest.

My date for the night was a nurse I'd been seeing for a month or so. Many times Gail would have to work late and since this was the time before cell phones, I found myself waiting outside her house, tossing a well-chewed tennis ball to her Springer spaniel, wondering when she would finally arrive. She pulled into the driveway so fast I thought that she was going through the closed garage door, but instead she stood on the brakes and the front end of that Mustang took a nosedive inches from the garage. There was a flurry of motion that looked much like a snowstorm as she jogged to her front door in her all-white nurse's uniform. Her blond hair fell onto her shoulders as she pulled off the little white hat that had been bobby pinned to her hair.

The Springer was ignoring her as he spun in circles waiting for me to throw the ball again. Instead, I followed the blizzard into the house. From the tangle of keys she'd left in her front door one would have thought that she was a night watchman. It wasn't hard to follow her trail; the white hat bounced off the couch and onto the floor along with her purse. Then, a shoe here and another there led the way to where her voice was trailing off as she revisited the events of the day about how slow the doctor had been with all the patients. I followed her toward the back of the house while holding the shoes that the Springer retrieved and dropped at my feet, waiting for me to throw.

Leaning against the wall in the hallway, I waited for her to change clothes, holding the shoes away from the dog that sat at my feet sweeping the hardwood floor with his tail.

Gail walked to the doorway holding a dress.

"Is this too floozy for where we're going?" she asked. She was down to her bra and white panty hose.

"No," I replied, not really looking at the dress. "You've got great legs. You might as well show them off."

She hooked her thumbs into the elastic waist of her white panty hose and pulled them down as she sat on the edge of her bed.

"Oh crap, look at the runs in these hose," she said as she pulled them off, wadding them up in a ball. I hadn't noticed the runs. She stood and tossed the hose in the general direction of a trash can. As she moved out of my view, I walked into her bedroom and retrieved the discarded hose. She turned to find me examining them.

"You know, if you were any other man, I'd think you were pretty kinky, but my best guess is that this has something to do with fly fishing," she said, peering over my shoulder.

"This will make a great seine," I replied. "It will fit over my stream net."

While few nurses wear white uniforms any more, you can buy the white panty hose at most supermarkets in those cute little egg-shaped packages. Tie a knot in the legs, cut off the bottom part of the legs, and slip the rest over your stream net. A safety pin will hold it on. Kick over a few rocks with your feet and use the net seine to capture what comes free in the drift.

You can always just turn over rocks or observe what's clinging

Caddisflies are often the predominate species on small streams as they seem to be less suspectible to adverse conditions such as drought.

to the rocks. A basic knowledge of these larvae-staged insects is very helpful at this point.

Caddis

Caddisflies are often the predominant order of aquatic insects in small streams. They are more adaptable to the sparse food and colder water temperatures that seem to be prevalent here. Turning over rocks or finding case makers by the thousands clinging to the tops of rocks is the norm. Everything from a size 20 to a size 8 is common. The Giant Orange Sedge, AKA October Caddis, is found in the Blackfoot River drainage and they are easy to spot because they are huge. My favorite dry fly pattern is a Deer Hair Caddis for the smaller sizes and the Bucktail Caddis for the larger ones.

There are two types of caddis larvae. One is the case builder and is very identifiable because it looks like small piles of tiny stones and detritus stuck together. The actual insect is inside and exposes its head and forelegs while crawling. The second type is

Various members of the Baetis family are very prevelant in these waters. Many high mountain lakes have blanket hatches of Callibaetis. A Parachute Adams is a great pattern choice.

a free-living larva that looks much like a small worm. After a closer look, preferably with a small magnifying glass, you'll see that the head has eyes and a distinct mouth. The tail has anal hooks and the body looks fuzzy. These larvae will range in size from a size 8 to a size 20.

Just prior to emergence, every caddis will build a case around itself to pupate. After their wings, legs, and antennae are in the nearly ready adult stage, they discard the pupal case and move to the surface where they dry their wings and fly. No caddis goes through a sub-adult stage like mayflies, but normally head to the brush for refuge after emergence. Shaking willows along stream banks will often result in clouds of flying caddis. Capture one for inspection as to size and color. Caddis adults have no tails and their four wings fold tent-like over their abdomens while at rest. After mating, caddis females will lay eggs in the stream by either

diving in the water or depositing the eggs on the surface to sink to the bottom.

Mayflies

Drakes, Pale Morning Duns, and Baetis are the most common mayfly species in these watersheds and all will catch the trout's interest when they hatch. A Parachute Adams in size 14 through 18 along with a Quigley Cripple in size 16 and 18 will cover most dry fly situations.

Fast moving streams tend to have various species of clinger, crawler, and swimmer mayflies but few burrowers. It's not critical to be able to recite family, genus, and species in order to catch fish, but it is valuable background information. Mayfly nymphs have two antennae, six legs, and two or three tails. Size can vary from a size 8 to a size 20 or even smaller.

Upon emergence, most mayflies will come to the surface, break open and crawl out of the nymphal shuck, dry their wings, and fly. This is the sub-adult dun stage. Before mating they must molt a thin coating to expose four clearer wings that replace the milky ones of the sub-adult. Mating is normally done in the air in swarms after which the females drop to the water to lay eggs and then die. Mayflies are "upwing" insects meaning that at rest the adult wings are almost perpendicular to their bodies. While mayflies have four wings, the hind wings are often so stunted you'll have to look closely to see them. The adults have either two or three tails.

Stoneflies

In the early summer you will often see golden stones in the size 8 range on the water or crawling on the banks and trees. On most high-country small streams, the trout don't seem to pay much attention to the larger patterns like #8 Yellow Stimulators. Instead they seem to key in on the Little Green or Little Yellow Stonefly patterns. These hatches happen throughout the entire summer and the numbers are very high compared to the hit and miss golden stones. I use the Deer Hair Caddis in a #16 or #18, but the smaller #18 works in about 90 percent of the situations you'll find. I've tried many other stonefly specific patterns, but none seem to work better than this easy-to-tie and easy-to-see caddis pattern.

Stonefly larvae will sometimes look very similar to mayfly nymphs. They have two antennae, six legs, and always two and never three tails. One differing characteristic is the wing pads that are more distinct than the mayfly's. After a closer look and study the differences become very apparent. Stoneflies are crawlers and clumsy swimmers. They don't pupate like caddis but instead migrate to shallower water to emerge by crawling out of the water onto rocks or logs. Then, after splitting the nymphal shuck, they dry their wings and look for a mate. The females lay eggs in several different ways depending on the species. Some lay eggs directly onto the stream's surface. Others deposit eggs on over-hanging branches and rocks. Then gravity pulls the eggs to the water and eventually to the bottom where they stick to the substrate and begin the cycle anew. Stonefly adults always have two tails and their four distinct wings fold flat over their abdomen while at rest. The larger ones fly with the grace of a Sumo wrestler on roller blades.

Midges

There are midge hatches even when the water temperatures are too cold to entice trout from the security of the wood-debris piles. It's rare that these westslope cutts will move just for a few midges. A #18 Griffiths Gnat or a #18 LaFontaine Buzzball will work on occasion but it's unusual that trout will take these patterns and not a small Parachute Adams. I find myself fishing these midge specific patterns only out of curiosity, not because they perform better.

Midge larvae looks much like a small housefly maggot from

While large stoneflies like this Salmonfly make fish crazy on large, lower-elevation rivers, they often get ignored in colder, high-country waters.

Some smaller streams are home to Skwalas.

which it is a close cousin. It's highly segmented and normally very small. Upon emergence the larvae moves to the surface where the adult crawls out. Midge adults have two wings that fold over their abdomen when at rest and no tails. Mating takes place soon after emergence and the females lay eggs on the surface and then die. On most freestone streams sizes will range between a size 20 down to a size 30 or smaller.

Terrestrials

While I carry a fly box with a large assortment of hopper, beetle, and ant patterns, it tends to stay out of the way in the back of my vest. It comes out when I see hoppers jumping around on the banks, but the terrestrial season seems to be fairly short in the high country and even throwing live grasshoppers in the water will only get fish to the surface under very specific conditions.

Generally speaking, trout on small, cold, mountain streams in western Montana will come out of hiding for specific hatches when the water temperature reaches that critical point to move

Hoppers may seem like a good pattern choice, but on many cold mountain streams they get ignored.

the insects. It seems to be the rare occasion that they will feed opportunistically on terrestrial patterns, especially large hopper patterns.

This was a puzzle for me because hopper patterns work wonderfully on larger rivers like the Blackfoot or Clark Fork. These patterns tend to be a requisite in other parts of the Rockies, but for reasons not entirely clear to me, they are largely ignored on most cold, high-mountain waters.

A small ant pattern will work when trout are actively and aggressively feeding on a hatch in progress, but the ant pattern won't often out perform the pattern that is specifically matched to the current hatch.

If you have a box of downwing patterns like the Deer Hair Caddis and a box of upwing patterns like Parachute Adams and Quigley Cripples, you'll be prepared for virtually any dry fly fishing opportunity you'll encounter.

Nymphs

There are going to be times when the trout stay closer to the bottom and not look up regardless of which dry fly pattern you float over their heads. When this occurs, you'll have to make a decision about what to do with this free-time opportunity. One option is to nymph fish.

I time my visits to these small streams to fish dry flies. I really love the visual aspect of top-water fly fishing. That moment when a trout breaches to take my fly adds an aspect to fly fishing that is lost when I'm blindly fishing weighted nymphs. I very much enjoy exploring these waters with a 2-weight rod and putting weighted nymphs and a strike indicator onto my leader dramatically changes the physics of my casting stroke. I find that I'm either forced to go to a heavier weight rod, or spend the entire time fighting the incompatibility of the two pieces of equipment. Over the years I've seen nymph fishermen out fish me almost every time, but for my personal tastes, I'm fishing for memories, not the body count. On many rivers, you'll certainly find me casting weighted nymphs or even large weighted streamers, but on these small streams it's like drinking a very old and delicate scotch whiskey out of a Styrofoam cup.

The two best patterns I have found for fishing with nymphs are a #16 or #18 Beadhead Prince Nymph and a #12 to #16 Beadhead Hare's Ear. There is a window when fish will take nymphs on the bottom and not dry flies on the surface. This is when the hatch is just beginning. You can get strikes if you run the nymphs very near or even under the wood debris or along undercut banks. If you are fishing these correctly, be prepared to lose a great deal of flies as they hang on the many branches and sunken logs.

While I'm not a huge fan of indicator-nymph fishing on these streams, I don't mind hanging a nymph dropper off my dry fly at times to coax fish out of their slumber and onto my flies. This two fly rig is much easier to cast with a 2-weight rod than a bobber, split shot, and weighted nymphs. A #18 Beadhead Peacock Soft Hackle at the beginning of a caddis hatch is deadly and a #18 Beadhead Lovebug works really well early on during a mayfly hatch. I drop these flies about 18 inches off the top dry fly and they often will not sink so far down the water column to prevent you from seeing the trout take it with a flash.

Wood piles are magnets for snagging weighted nymphs, making dry fly fishing the technique of choice.

CHAPTER FIVE

High Country Perils

Back in the 1960s, America seemed like a very safe place. Gas prices were stable and for around 30 cents a gallon a guy in a uniform would pump it for you and check the engine. The Ruskies put a bunch of missiles in Cuba, but it was downplayed in my life, and I knew I could hide under my desk if the missiles were headed for my school. Life was predictable and I was very comfortable living in my small town in southern Colorado where two teenaged boys could take their dog and hunt pheasants by themselves. Like many other young men, I thought no harm would ever come to me and I would live forever.

It was very cold, even for late fall. Sitting on the edge of my bed I pulled on my waffle-weave cotton long johns. They came out of the dryer three sizes too small and my recent growth spurt made matters worse. My jeans were also too short but the bloodstains from my recent deer hunt hadn't washed out and I wasn't going to use them for anything but hunting anyway. The wool sweater my mom knitted would keep me warm under my canvas hunting coat and I was ready when Smitty showed up at my house. Hemo was already whining as he paced from window to window in the back seat of the old Plymouth. Hemo was a Weimaraner who bled a lot when they cut off his tail, so he became "Hemophiliac" which we of course shortened to

In addition to the normal perils like slippery rocks or steep hillsides, fly fishing away from the crowds requires the angler to give more attention to safety issues.

just Hemo. I threw my gear in the trunk but held the cased shotgun in the front seat with me.

Smitty drove like he was auditioning for Chuck Yeager's test pilot job, leaving the normal vapor trail behind us as we left Canon City on the four-lane headed east. The Troggs were belting out "Wild Thing" on the radio as we finally slid to a stop off the gravel road.

Wild thing, you make my heart sing,
You make everything, groovey!

My heart may have been racing as a consequence of Smitty's driving. Or maybe it was the anticipation of the hunt, but when I opened the car door I was struck in the face by the blast of cold air and assaulted from the rear seat by Hemo jumping over my shoulder and onto the snow-covered ground. He immediately began sniffing.

The hunting was slow. We walked all the usual places and although we saw fresh rabbit tracks, we didn't put up any ringnecks. Close to noon we were getting antsy enough to shoot a cottontail, just to put something in our vests. Hemo was out front as

Thimbleberries are a great afternoon snack for the angler as well as bears. They usually ripen in August but use caution when approaching these patches.

we worked our way along the dry irrigation ditch. This elevated ditch was high enough so that I couldn't see Smitty on the other side, but we'd hunted together so often that I pretty well knew his pace. I heard him shoot and ran up the ditch bank to see if maybe I could get a second shot at one of the birds.

Approaching the top of the berm I saw several things all at once. The rooster was flying directly at me but very low. Hemo was sprinting about five yards behind him and Smitty had pulled his shotgun up to take the bird. The muzzle of that 12-gauge lifted and I knew it was going to hurt. I got most of my back toward him when the spray hit me.

"Shit, Smitty!" I screamed as my legs were suddenly on fire from the pellets. I turned around to see numerous tiny dots of red expanding on my jeans.

In a moment he was running toward me yelling something about how sorry he was.

"I'm going to kick your ass!" I yelled as he got to me.

"Are you ok?" He was near panic, which was totally out of character for him.

"Yeah, I'm ok I guess. But man does that burn." The sting was actually subsiding a little bit by then but as I pulled up my jeans and long johns I realized that the area around the pellets was numb. My first thought was that I couldn't go home like that because Smitty's dad would be really pissed at him. Not to mention what my dad was going to say.

"You have to go to the doctor," Smitty declared. His father was my dentist so of course I wasn't going to argue with his obviously superior medical knowledge. It took him a while to convince me but we packed up and made a very ambulance-like trip to the hospital.

I don't remember much about the time at our small rural hospital except the sound of each pellet as it bounced on the bottom of a glass beaker every time the doctor extracted one from my legs. My sweater and heavy coat prevented all but a couple from hitting my back so mostly they were confined to the back of my legs. Later I was able to convince my mom that I was walking funny because of a twisted ankle.

On some streams there seems to be many more obstacles than water.

We tend to live in an illusionary world. We see ourselves as Lord and Master of our earthly domain. We live in climate-controlled houses and drive cars with cruise control and CD players. Our work places are, for the most part, safe and clean. We point at the sky and declare that direction "up." We point to the ground and declare that direction "down." We ignore the fact that we live on a sphere and there is no "up" or "down." The sun does not revolve around the earth and we are not the center of the universe. We are in fact susceptible to injury or death every moment of every day. We just choose to ignore that little fact because if we fixated on it, we'd never leave the house. But then people die in their houses of heart attacks and falls.

Being out in the woods, especially if you do it alone, presents a certain amount of risk I feel drawn to. There's a chance that I'll fall off a cliff, take a spill in a stream and be swept under a pile of logs, or get attacked by an animal. It's all possible; it's not likely as I go to great lengths to prepare myself for the unexpected,

Learn to identify bear scat and be alert when you find it.

but still possible. People do get lost in the woods and some are never found. It happens, even though statistically you're much more likely to die driving than fishing.

When fishing alone in the high country, it's a good idea to admit that the earth and nature could swallow you up and no one would ever hear from you again. If you grab your chest at your desk, someone will dial 9-1-1 and professionally trained medical staff will administer drugs and a defibrillator to save your life. If you fall and break your leg stepping over a wet log in the wilderness, you're on your own unless you always fish with an EMT or ER doctor. If you become lost, injured, or ill, it may be days before you are found.

There is a way to hedge your bet and maximize your safety while fishing in remote locations, and that is to be prepared.

While it's true that we humans have opposing digits and can make tools and weapons, our best weapon will always be our brain. You can't outrun or outfight a grizzly bear and a tiny tick can penetrate your skin and make you sick. Giardia will turn your large intestine into an amusement park and the sun can blind you. Knowledge is key. It won't add weight to your vest and once you have it, you don't have to worry about leaving it behind in the hotel room.

Bears

Two different species of bears call Montana home – the grizzly or brown bear (*Ursus arctos*) and the black bear (*Ursus americanus*). It's very important to know the difference because your response to an encounter will be very different depending on the species. Two great books on this subject are *Bear Attacks – Their Causes and Avoidance* by Stephen Herrero and *Lives of Grizzlies, Montana and Wyoming* by Jim Cole.

What I've learned about bears from both reading and experience is that they have very individual personalities and their demeanor will vary depending on the circumstances. Grizzly bears will fight to protect themselves, their young, their kill, or their territory. Black bears are much more likely to abandon all of the above. Statistics show that the chances of being killed by a bear are infinitesimal. Often this is compared to being struck by lightening. Like most statistics, this one doesn't really tell the entire story because few will people ever see a grizzly, much less be killed by one. Their range, at least in the lower 48 states, is mostly limited to western Montana. But as you venture into the grizzly's backyard in Montana's wilderness areas, you should know that your chances of an encounter just rocketed off the statistician's chart. All of the recorded grizzly bear attacks in the lower 48 states over last 50 years have occurred in or around western Montana.

Many biologists estimate that the number of grizzly bears in the lower 48 states is less than 1,000 animals. In the summer and fall of 2004 when I was taking many of the photos for this book, I saw nine different grizzly bears. In the summer of 2005, I saw only one grizzly even though I spent more days in their territory than in 2004. I believe the reason is that 2005 was a more normal precipitation year. Yes, I know that this is a very limited sample, and this is anecdotal evidence, but the differences were dramatic. Grizzlies are high-country, solitary animals, but diminished food supplies will move them into areas with higher densities of humans. Some of these great bears are now conditioned to the sound of a rifle shot during big game season because it means a gut-pile banquet.

Don't be terrorized by bears. Each of the encounters I've had has been exhilarating and never once did I feel like I was in mortal danger. I don't chase grizzlies for a photo and I leave the area when I see them. I don't carry firearms because I don't want to kill bears and any firearm large enough to drop a charging bear is way more weight than I'm willing to carry. I choose instead to use caution and awareness and the ultimate weapon, my brain.

There are many myths about bears. The biggest one is that you can outrun a bear if you run downhill. I've seen bears run downhill at a pace that would challenge a Kentucky Derby winner. Black bears can climb trees easily and quickly. Grizzly cubs can climb trees, but the adult isn't really adept at it. Still, most experts say you should be at least 35 feet off the ground to be safe from a grizzly.

Unless you own a Karelian, your dog is more likely to first chase or harass a bear, and then, when the bear turns on him, your best friend will race to the shelter of your legs, angry bear in tow. That new 2-weight rod is no defense for a several hundred pound highly irritated bear.

If a grizzly attacks and knocks you to the ground, play dead. When you are no longer a threat it will likely leave. If a black bear attacks, fight with anything you've got. Never run unless you are dead certain that you can reach safety before the bear reaches you. Recently, on the recommendation of Jim Cole, I began to

These live bear traps are a warning there is a problem bear in the area that the Montana Fish Wildlife & Parks Deparment is trying to catch.

A very serene scene like this one at Snowbank Lake can quickly change into an afternoon thunderstorm accompanied by strong winds, rain, or hail.

carry Counter Assault pepper spray. It's light, non-lethal, and has proven to deter attacks from both grizzly and black bears. It's made in the heart of bear country in Kalispell, Montana. If you buy this product, be sure to check with airline regulations before packing it in your bag. It may not be permissible to take it on the plane. It's easy to use and comes with a carrying case that fits easily on a wading belt. There are other brands of pepper spray available, but from my research they either lack the active ingredient Capsaicin in sufficient concentration (>1.5%) to adequately deter an attack or don't have the requisite propellant to deliver the pepper far enough (>25 feet) or long enough (>5 seconds). Counter Assault was the only product to meet all the guidelines established by the federal Interagency Grizzly Bear Committee.

I am convinced that the pepper spray is actually a great defense for deterring a bear, but I'm not one to walk through the woods or along a trout stream singing or whistling away the bears. I don't wear "bear bells." The reason is that I've been in many situations where a buddy was standing on one side of a fast moving stream and I was on the other less than 20 feet apart, and I could not hear him no matter how loudly he yelled. So unless you're willing to walk the high country with a 100db compressed-air horn, I'm not convinced that sound, especially singing or bells, will be heard by the bear at a distance great enough to deter an attack.

Bears are individuals. The most dangerous ones are those who have had human contact and been rewarded with food. No two bears will respond identically to a situation. Any advice you get from books or experts only works some of the time.

Be prepared, get educated, and be cautious. Bears are always looking for easy food and their sense of smell is legendary. If you get a whiff of or see a dead animal, be very cautious as carrion attracts bears. If you observe any group of scavenging birds that may be feeding on a carcass, be very careful, or find another fishing spot. Patches of huckleberries, thimbleberries, and raspberries are food sources that bears remember and even teach their young to find. I too feast on these delightful treats but only after a careful and slow approach.

Garter snakes are commonly found in high-country environments. While rare, rattlesnakes have been encountered in these same habitats.

There are two enduring bear jokes in Montana:
Never go into bear country with someone you can't outrun.
And
Q: How do you tell the difference between black bear scat and grizzly scat?
A: Black bear scat has pieces of root, berries, and nuts. Grizzly scat has silver bells and smells like pepper spray.

Other Critters

Wood ticks are a much more likely problem for the fly fisher. In the Rockies the prime tick season is the spring when things are wetter. As soon as the woods dry up and warm up, the ticks seem to vanish. A careful self-examination at the end of the day is in order. Your scalp, but particularly the area where your hat meets your hair, seems to be the area where I find most of these annoying little parasites. A fine-toothed comb will generally remove them from your hair if you find them before they have bored into your skin, which usually takes several hours.

If you do find a deeply embedded tick, you will have to remove it to prevent infection or worse. A careful steady hand can grab the tick and gently pull it out. Methods like burning an embedded tick with a match or covering it with nail polish are bad ideas because it often causes the tick to empty its stomach contents into your blood stream. The current theory is that most tick-related disease isn't transmitted for 24 hours, so a careful nightly check is important.

Most people don't respond to a moose with shivers up their spine, but maybe they should. Moose are very large and can inflict serious injury on humans. Give them a lot of room and realize that they seem to be the most ill-tempered animals in the woods, especially a cow moose with a calf. Don't crowd them for any reason.

Waterfalls like this one in Glacier National Park often create slippery footing, but the fishing always seems to make the slow moving worth it.

Encounters with rattlesnakes are almost unheard of in the Rocky Mountain high country but fairly common in the lower, rolling hills. Forget what you've seen in old westerns about aggressive rattlers as this is a very timid and slow-to-attack creature. You may not always hear the rattles before you see them, however. Many times snakes, even vipers, will bite without injecting venom. If you are within a few hours of a hospital, my best suggestion is to forego snakebite kits, but especially forget what you've seen in cowboy movies about cutting an "X" into the bite to suck it out. One emergency room doctor said to me, "Do you really think you can suck venom out of someone's bloodstream?" Instead, transport the person to a hospital after removing any jewelry or watches because the first symptom to occur is usually swelling. While few people die of snakebites, the venom can cause significant nerve and tissue damage if not treated quickly.

I was a fly-fishing guide for years in Montana and Colorado. I've only seen a few dozen rattlesnakes while guiding. After every encounter, the subject of snakebite first aid always came up, especially on remote, five-day Smith River trips. After I explained that rattlesnakes don't like to waste their venom and that only 35 to 50 percent of those bit ever get envenomated and only about one in a thousand of those envenomated die, people still wonder "what if." "What if I'm far from a hospital, with no phone or means to call for help, and I get bit by a rattlesnake?"

For the curious, here's what I've been able to figure out from data collected from medical people who regularly work in remote areas. Keep in mind there isn't 100 percent agreement on this subject.

First, immobilize the bitten extremity, clean the wound and transport the victim. If you have a Sawyer Extractor kit, apply it to the punctures within five minutes. This should remove about

Navigating through thick brush and downfall, plus steep drops, can be a challenge to many anglers.

35 percent of the venom if indeed the snake envonomated the person. Quickly remove all tight fitting or restrictive jewelry. Watch for signs of shock like heavy sweating, clammy skin, or shallow breathing. Often, symptoms will not appear for at least two hours.

Without professional medical care the envenomated person will get very sick and could incur serious nerve or tissue damage or even death. I never had a client who was bitten, but if I had I wouldn't mess around with extractor kits, I would transport him to a hospital.

Lightning

The Rocky Mountain states have the highest per-capita lightning fatality rate of anywhere in the country except Florida. Standing in a stream waving a graphite rod during a lightning storm puts an angler in danger. The vast majority of lightning-caused deaths occur on boats because a boat on the water is almost always the highest object around. If you find yourself in the middle of a storm, get out of the stream and retreat to a low spot like a slight ravine. Tall trees may offer some protection from the rain, but they are a target for lightning and should be avoided.

If lightning is striking in your immediate area and there is no reasonable shelter, lay your rod flat on the ground 30 feet or more from you. Then, with your feet together and your knees bent, crouch with your chest down to your thighs and your hands over the back of your neck. This is referred to as the lightning desperation position. Do not lay flat on the ground as lightning can travel through the earth. Keep away from anything metallic like fences.

Cars are good lightning shelters as long as you are not touching any metal. Tents, because of the metal poles, are zero protection from lightning.

Hypothermia

Hypothermia is likely the most dangerous and the most prevalent problem facing the lone angler on small streams in western Montana. As a longtime fly-fishing guide, I treated people for hypothermia more than any other single thing. One of the first symptoms of hypothermia is disorientation, which is especially dangerous if you are alone and fishing an unfamiliar stream.

Carrying a raincoat on a day that begins very warm without a cloud in the sky seems unnecessary, but many times an afternoon squall will move in, and the wind increases with the downdrafts, and then it begins to rain. If you are dry and protected from the wind, you've won three-quarters of the battle. If the event lasts for more than a few minutes, the temperature will drop. If you have a raincoat, you're probably going to enjoy the fishing for the rest of the day. If not, you'll be walking back to your vehicle cold and wet. The bottom line to preventing hypothermia is staying dry and dressing in layers that wick away moisture from your skin.

If someone is displaying the early signs of hypothermia such as severe shivering, bluish or blotchy skin, numbness or tingling sensations, it's best to catch it before it advances. Advanced symptoms include disorientation, decreased coordination, difficulty moving limbs, and a slowed pulse. As the core body temperature drops, the victim often stops shivering.

Get the victim dry, out of the elements if possible, and warm. How you warm them is important, as you want to warm their core first. Apply heat to their neck, underarms, and groin. Because in this condition their heart is very vulnerable, it's important not to jar the victim. Severe cases should have a follow-up medical exam because a drastic drop in body core temperatures can cause damage to the heart and other internal organs.

There are many other injuries that could occur in the backcountry from allergic reactions to certain plants like poison ivy to stings from insects. The ones listed above are pointed out because they seem to be overlooked. Someone who is susceptible to altitude sickness will likely be aware of this before they embark on a backcountry fishing trip. Caring for wounds due to cuts, broken bones, or CPR is something more appropriately learned in a first-aid class. Take the time to learn these valuable skills and put together a good first-aid kit. Having the confidence and the knowledge to help someone injured in the backcountry is a great skill to possess. ⌒

Hypothermia will often be your biggest concern. Go prepared and enjoy the day!

CHAPTER SIX

Cottonwood Creek
The Sleeper

I found these four streams using the methods described in this book. I got topos and maps, I searched the Internet, and then I went to the state library and found the biologist's data. I drove to the streams where I used my insect seine to sample the water for aquatic larvae and then I looked at the streamside foliage for the adults. I then fished the waters. My approach was very methodical, and the results of getting wonderful photographs and catching hundreds of trout bordered on a mystical experience. The entire journey was one of wondrous exploration.

It was mostly a solo journey. I called on friends from time to time to join me so that I could have some people in the photos. Sharing what I found with special friends was very enjoyable, but those moments of exploring even after I did my homework and was pretty confident that I'd catch trout were moments brazened into my memory, mine forever.

A short time after my first book *Fly Fishing Montana's Missouri River* came out, a guy came up to me in the parking lot of a fly shop. He asked, "Are you Trapper?" "Yup," I replied. "Did you write that book about the Missouri?" "Yes, I did," I answered. "But you gave away all the secrets," he said with a hint of anger in his voice. I said, "You mean the secrets everyone around here already knows about?" "Yes," he shot back.

Cottonwood Creek doesn't look like much of a trout stream as you casually drive by on your way to the Blackfoot River. Then one day a hatch is on and fish are rising all around.

There are likely very few secret fishing spots in the lower 48 states. Someone has fished every one of them. There are many places that are lightly fished and there are many places that people either write off as too small or likely private or some other reason. Find these places on your own and you have earned the right to fish them even if others mistakenly declare them "theirs."

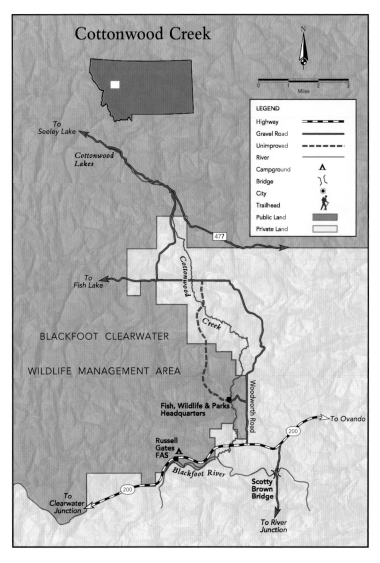

This territorial stance we take up about fishing spots is pretty interesting, especially on federal or state lands. Here in Montana there have been numerous court challenges to landowners who believe they own the river and the water that runs down it. Some think that no one has the right to breathe their air or float on their water. Even when the courts tell them they are wrong, they come back with even more lawyers and legal briefs. When that doesn't work they put barbed-wire fences across rivers and streams. They run people off and sometimes threaten them physically. All this because they think they have ownership where they don't.

No one owns a secret fishing spot on public land, and even if you follow the path I've presented in this book and find a spot where the fish are big and stupid and there isn't a cigarette butt or boot track, you still don't own it. If someone happens to approach as you are sight-casting to rising fish on a little known stream, I ask that you treat them as a kindred spirit, not as a foul interloper. Know that if they ventured off the beaten path and pushed their way through heavy brush to fish a small stream, they are not your enemy, but more like you than different. I ask that you share what you learned with them, just as I have shared what I've learned with you. I ask that you leave no trash, no empty beer cans, and no cigarette butts on our (yours and mine) streams, but instead treat these fragile fisheries with a certain reverence.

After a few years of drought I was very worried about the small streams in the Blackfoot River drainage. These streams are hit from both ends in times of drought. During the summer months these small streams depend on snow pack in the mountains many miles away to continue flowing. Spring and summer rain will help because often that rain keeps irrigators from pulling water from the stream. As the water levels drop, the water temperatures go up and the problem is compounded. But some, like Cottonwood Creek, are lucky enough to have a few lakes nursing them and during drought they suckle from their mothers for their lives.

It was late August and as I sat on the picnic table in front of the old ranch house on the Clearwater-Blackfoot Game Range, there was room for a bit of guarded optimism. Our snow pack

Cottonwood Creek runs through a variety of environments from marshy to more conventional water.

from the previous winter wasn't great, but spring and summer rains along with temperatures on the cool side left most of my watery buddies in pretty good shape. This particular parking area is deserted most of the year, but during the summer months it's a bustle of activity from the many college students who reside here to study elk and grizzly bears. When I attended college I spent my summers working in a department store, so I will always remain envious of these young soon-to-be biologists.

Scurrying among them was tiny Mavis Lorenz. Mavis, even in her late 70s, showed little sign of slowing down. She was there to help these youngsters with their research and few will ever spend as many days outside as this matriarch. During each encounter I've had with Mavis she never failed to remind me, "You don't need testosterone to pull a trigger." Mavis has shot, skinned, and hauled more trophy big-game animals out of the Montana wilderness than anyone I know. She's listed in the Boone and Crocket record books and her mounts decorate stores all over western Montana. While she always loves sharing her extensive knowl-

This wonderful little stream is overgrown with willows in places, which discourages many anglers. These same willows create a near-perfect habitat for the resident trout.

edge of the outdoors with young people, she normally hunts alone, just as she did as a child.

Mavis was relating a hunt she'd had in the boonies of the Yukon for bighorn sheep. Just as she was getting to the good part, one of the college kids announced he was ready to set out DNA traps for grizzlies. In a flurry, amidst apologies, she was in the truck, bouncing down the dirt road that hadn't seen a road grader since Elvis was touring. She was driving; the kid in the seat next to her was frantically trying to find his seatbelt. If you fish this stream, drop in and say hello to Mavis.

Cottonwood Creek is a wonderful little hidden area. From the road it looks like a private ranch even though the signs clearly show it is state land.

In 1948 the Montana Fish, Wildlife & Parks Department, using monies collected from licenses, bought the Boyd ranch and created the Clearwater-Blackfoot Wildlife Management Area. The locals call this the "Game Range." This public area is well over 100 square miles with enough fishable water to keep anyone busy for a lifetime or two.

Many of the streams and lakes in this area are well known and easy to access. Consequently, they get the most pressure. Cottonwood Creek is a sleeper. On the lower end, just before it dumps into the Blackfoot River near the campground at Russell Gates Fishing Access Site, it meanders through a wetlands looking more suited for waterfowl hunting than fly fishing.

One of the first clues about this stream could easily come from simply looking at a map. Immediately it's apparent that this stream flows out of the high country and into a major river. Whenever this happens it might as well have a huge neon sign on it that says "Great Fishing Here." The angler who is willing to bushwhack through some thick willows and deal with some silty ground will be rewarded with several species of trout, including rainbow, westslope cutthroat, hybrids, browns, bull trout, and brookies. Sometimes you can find all of these species in the same run or hole.

These trout are phantoms. When water temperatures are colder than high 40s, the stream seems to be void of life with only an occasional small fish here and there. Then, like a magical switch, the hatch begins and pods of marauding trout cruise the holes and beaver ponds looking for prey. It's all about timing the hatch. A good rule of thumb is that cold, drizzly days aren't going to be very productive. The down side is that on bright, sunny days a careless angler is going to spook every fish in the stream. Use the brush to hide from the fish. Careful casters will be rewarded and fast moving waders will be punished.

Over the course of the summer months you'll see hatches of midges, mayflies, caddis, and stoneflies, but probably the predominant hatch is caddis. Caddis and the many small stonefly hatches are very similar in profile and size, so a great choice is a Deer Hair Caddis. Add an upwing pattern like a Parachute Adams and a Quigley Cripple and it's really about all you'll need, but few fly fishers will push through all those willows with only one fly box. The backup flies should include a few nymphs and soft hackles for those desperate times, in addition to a terrestrial box with hoppers and ants. Often, when the fishing is off due to lack of hatches and unfavorable water temperatures, the fish won't be lured out of their hiding places with anything short of a Dupont Spinner.

Browns, rainbows, cutthroats, brook trout, and bull trout all reside in Cottonwood Creek.

CHAPTER SEVEN

Monture Creek
Near Wilderness Experience

Rick Oie and I have fished together for several years on many different rivers. When I suggested we float Monture Creek from the campground down to the Russell Gates Fishing Access Site on the Big Blackfoot, he was all over it. We even decided to take along our wives. We'd both fished different sections of this stream but neither of us had worked our way up to the campground from the Blackfoot because it's nearly two miles up and a long walk back. Floating seemed like a good option, especially since recent rains had raised the flows in this small stream.

As I stepped out of my truck, my Tevas sunk into cold mud past my ankles. One look at the water and our hopes of big trout eating salmonflies quickly faded. It looked like the only thing we were going to hook was one of the Washington Monument-sized logs that quickly floated by us. Still, the day started off sunny with the temperature near 60 degrees and because we're both hardcore optimists, our boxes of salmonflies were kept at the ready. It turned out to be an adventure of a different sort.

The campground really isn't set up for launching any sort of boat or raft but with a little wrangling we had both rafts in the water with wives and gear on board. From the time we left the campground it was apparent that this was going to be more of a boat ride than a serious fishing trip. Neither of our

Monture Creek begins in the Scapegoat Wilderness and delivers very cold water to the Blackfoot River.

wives was experienced enough on the oars to handle this fast moving torrent with so many obstacles, so the notion that Rick and I could fish from the moving rafts faded quickly from our minds.

Whenever you float a new section of stream for the first time, it's always a bit unnerving because you're constantly vigilant for barbed-wire fences strung across the river, waterfalls that didn't show up on the topo map, diversion dams, or bank-to-bank dead-

falls. These snags can pull the raft underwater and hold it there. What you don't expect is a hazard from overhead.

We were moving downstream in the fast water that was rising with the recent rains. Our pace rivaled the average Indy car when we turned a corner to find a footbridge spanning the creek. I slowed the raft by back rowing while trying to eyeball the clearance versus the height of raft. The banks were steep and a portage around the low bridge would be very tough; getting the raft stuck under the bridge with Shirley and me in it would be even worse.

"Trapper, we aren't going to fit under there are we," she asked, trying to hide her anxiety.

"Oh, no problem," I replied with the confidence of Neil Armstrong. "We'll have plenty of clearance."

I directed Shirley to get to the bottom of the raft as I lined it up in the center of the creek and started under the bridge.

"Man, this going to be close," I muttered under my breath.

"What did you say Trapper?" asked the voice from the bottom of the raft.

"I said we'll have plenty of room honey." I was shipping in the oars and doing a last minute assessment all the while knowing that we were already committed and there was no turning back.

From my position in the bottom of the raft I helplessly watched the tube of the bow miss the weathered wood of the underside of the bridge by an inch or so, but the back tube had a seat mount on it. As we drifted the raft turned slightly. I looked back to see the seat mount scrape empty salmonfly shucks from the bottom of the bridge. The raft stuttered and then released.

"See, no problem," I declared, happy that she couldn't have seen how close we had come to disaster.

As we drifted out into the broken sunshine, my first thought was to Rick and Jill who were a few

Monture Creek

LEGEND

Highway	▬▬▬
Gravel Road	———
River	———
Campground	⛺
Bridge	)(
City	◉
Trailhead	🚶
Public Land	▬▬
Private Land	▭

Monture Creek Recreation Site

477

Monture Creek

Monture Road

Monture Creek Campground

To Clearwater Junction — 200

Scotty Brown Bridge

Ovando — 200 — To Lincoln

Blackfoot River

To River Junction

Sometimes large piles of brush can be a hinderence, but the resident cutthroat trout could not exist here without this shelter.

Upper Monture Creek is home to tall conifers, thickets of thimbleberries, and cutthroat trout that often hide under overhanging banks.

minutes behind us. I yelled a caution to Rick who saw the bridge just before my warning. His raft sat lower in the water but there were two strung rods hanging off the stern. Rick was taking a mental inventory and seemed to suddenly remember the rods. He turned around and pulled them in just before the raft's bow was sliding under the bridge, which they cleared by four or five inches.

After a portage or two around bank-to-bank snags we were at the mouth of the creek on the Big Blackfoot River. The Big B was running bank full and it began to rain. The wind was hauling sheets of water from the river, mixing it with the rain, and dumping it on our heads. Even in the heavy current it was a huge wet hand that pushed us back upstream. We live for these adventures, but it was nice when we finally had the rafts onto the trailers at the Russ Gates Campground and were in our trucks with the heaters going full blast. It's times like these that answer questions about why the divorce rate among guides is so high.

Monture Creek begins deep in the old growth forests of the

Bob Marshall Wilderness in western Montana. It gathers water from snowmelt and several smaller streams on its 24-mile journey to the Blackfoot River. Once there, this water will move through the Clark Fork, mingle with the vast water of the Columbia River, and eventually empty into the Pacific Ocean. Some of the old folks remember Pacific salmon being caught in some of these remote Montana streams, but that was before dams and other man-made barriers thwarted the salmon runs.

Throughout its course, about half of this creek runs through private land devoted mostly to raising cattle. Over the last couple of decades generous landowners have assisted several groups to restore this small stream through bank restoration and many other projects. The result has been to allow native bull trout to migrate freely from the Blackfoot to traditional spawning grounds in the upper reaches. These fragile fish are on the threatened species list. Now they are making a very slow and precarious comeback. They deserve special consideration and tender loving care if hooked by the angler. In fact, the Montana Fish, Wildlife & Parks Department has made intentional fishing for them illegal, and if you do hook one, you are mandated to return it to the water immediately. If you read the regulations you will note that it doesn't say immediately after you take a roll of pictures. The photograph in this book was taken with special permission from FWP with the intention of educating people as to what this rare native trout looks like. They have been mistaken for large brook trout or even lake trout. Bull trout begin to migrate to spawning areas during late summer and spawn during the early fall. Be ultra aware of the redds if you are fishing this stream during those spawning times. Although it's of little interest to fly fishers, it is illegal to fish with anything but artificial flies and lures within 100 yards of the mouth of Monture Creek and the Blackfoot River to protect bull trout and westslope cutthroats.

Monture is really divided into two sections. The lower section is only a few miles long, from Highway 200 to the Blackfoot River. Access can be gained from the campground just off the highway, or by driving to the Scotty Brown Bridge and then walking upstream a short distance to the mouth of the creek. Much of the adjacent land along the creek in this section is private property. Montana stream access laws allow you to fish and wade below the normal high water mark, but it's illegal to trespass across private land to get to or from the stream. As mentioned before, this section can be floated early in the season but much will depend on current drought conditions and water flow. This section fishes much like the Blackfoot. You'll find rainbows and browns more abundant here than in the upper reaches where the predominant species is westslope cutthroat. These native cutts are also on the threatened list, so anywhere you catch them in the Blackfoot drainage they must be immediately returned to the water.

The upper section of Monture is all within the Lolo National Forest. Parts of it north of Highway 200 are private. Keep in mind that this is prime bear country and precautions described in Chapter 3 should be reviewed prior to heading into this area. Here the openness of the lower reaches is gone and replaced with old growth trees of mostly Douglas-fir. The undergrowth makes getting to the stream nearly impossible at times. Break down your rod and you'll get there with something to fish with. Fishing here is easy; getting through all the brush, wood debris piles, and downed trees is tough.

Fly selection is fundamental. Upwing and downwing patterns in two different colors of olive and ginger will fit most situations. Presentations must be precise and delicate. Often you'll have to risk losing a fly in order to catch a rising trout that is hiding between two downed logs. When the fish takes your fly that extra backbone in your rod will come

in handy to turn it away from the sunken debris. Prepare yourself to lose this battle frequently. When the fish are more interested in food just below the surface, drop a Peacock Soft Hackle off your dry for the caddis hatches or a Lovebug for the mayflies.

Often, on many small streams in the western states, it's not necessary to get very far from the road or your car to find rising fish.

CHAPTER EIGHT

North Fork of the Blackfoot
A Wilderness Experience

Women's intuition. My mom certainly had it. She could use it remotely by calling from another part of the house "Son, I didn't send you to your room to read your new *Field & Stream*, you are there to pick up your clothes." Back then there were no video cameras, so I could only conclude that her superpowers were genuine. This mysterious ability worked best when she took up her Superman stance with her hands on her hips, standing defiantly in front of me. She could spot a fabrication faster than the Man of Steel looking through an ordinary door with his x-ray vision. When she ordered me to look her in the eye, I knew that I'd been rendered defenseless, so in response, I would just stand there, staring at my shoes until she lifted my chin and I was face to face with the judge, jury, and if need be, executioner.

Many of the TV shows of the late 1950s had police themes and sometimes I'd watch some cop trying to get information from a suspect and wondered why they didn't just send in my mom. I could see her walking into the precinct stationhouse.

"Good morning Mrs. Badovinac." The desk sergeant was tipping his hat as he stood to greet her. She was opening her purse and extracting a tissue as she walked through the door courteously opened by a uniformed policeman.

Much of the North Fork of the Blackfoot requires some effort to reach it. This horse bridge is more than three miles from the trailhead. The views alone are well worth the hike.

"Thank you, young man," she said kindly to the officer and then turned toward the desk and threw a reply that direction. "Good morning, Sergeant." Her stiff dress stood far from her body and made a soft grinding sound as she strolled toward the interrogation room, snapping her purse shut. Her sensible shoes made a distinct tap each time her heel hit the hardwood floor. Her clip-on earrings were robin shell blue and were slipped off whenever she needed to talk on the phone.

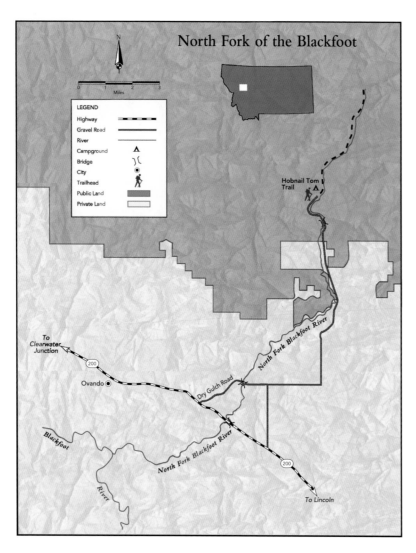

A few polite taps on the door and the detective unlocked it from the other side by inserting a large metal key into the oblong shaped hole below the knob. She glided into the room holding her purse with both hands. Another detective was rolling down his sleeves. He picked up his hat and as he walked by, paused, and whispered, "This is a tough one. You want we should stay in here wit' cho?"

"Detective, I have four large sons. Most of the time they are armed with high-powered big game rifles or shotguns along with very sharp knives and various handguns. I think I can handle one young man." She put her purse on the table and finger-by-finger removed her dress gloves. The suspect slouched defiantly with a Lucky Strike behind his ear. His well-lubed hair was combed into a duck-ass haircut. One leg was crossed, putting his ankle on the knee of the other. Rolled-up jeans exposed a pack of cigarettes in his white sock and he kept on his black leather jacket even in the summer heat. One arm was draped over the back of the chair as he defiantly chewed gum, smacking it with an open mouth, all useless bravado. Mom stood over him in the Superman stance.

"Look at me, young man." Her head was cocked ever so slightly to the side.

"I don't wanna'," he replied, looking at his shoes and picking an imaginary speck of lint off his sock.

"Young man . . ." Her voice trailed off as she lifted his chin and looked into his eyes.

The effect was immediate. "I did it. I did it," he blurted out. His face was contorted as he sobbed like a schoolgirl with a skinned knee.

My mom wouldn't have needed rubber hoses or polygraphs; she'd have done it just with her intuitive powers.

Years later I drove into the parking lot of an old beer joint called Montana Al's where I was to meet a woman and her boyfriend. The deal was that I'd show them a great place to fish and disburse some fly-fishing tips, and they would sign a photo release so that I could use their images for my book or future articles.

There are plenty of runs like this one on the North Fork.

The parking lot was empty except for an old muddy pickup. I could see the boots of some cowboy hanging out the passenger-side window. He'd likely closed the bar only hours before and wisely chose to sleep in his truck rather than braving the challenge of the open road and a DUI.

Kerry turned her Nissan pickup into the gravel parking lot and came to a stop next to me. She shut off the engine and started removing gear from the jump seat. As she got out of the truck I could see that she was young, pretty, and alone. I figured she'd eventually tell me why the boyfriend wasn't there.

It was time for the Reverse Women's Intuition Maneuver. As I walked toward her I removed my sunglasses and looked her in the eyes so that she could see that I wasn't lying when I said, "I'm happy to finally meet you." She could see, and her women's intuition would confirm, that I wasn't a threat to her. She was about to get into my truck and drive about 60 miles to the North Fork of the Blackfoot. There she would get out of my truck and accompany me into the Scapegoat Wilderness. She'd do all this with a man she didn't even know. Her intuition had to be in top working order and I wasn't going to make her ask to look into my eyes.

Later that day she said she knew right off I was harmless. At my age it would have been good for my ego if it had taken her a bit longer.

This late August day was gray, and gray is not good for photos. We left the Hobnail Tom Trailhead at the North Fork Campground about 9 A.M. She with rod and about 500 of my flies divided into three boxes, me with over 50 pounds of cameras and tripod. Sometimes the toughest decision you'll make all day is what to carry and what to leave behind. Kerry was asking me this and ended up opting for wearing a small fishing hip pack and carrying a good-sized backpack which she hid a mile or two into the hike.

Fall was edging its way into the high country. There were still a few thimbleberries around but they'd been picked over by critters and fishermen so there wasn't much more than a taste left for us.

After hiking almost two miles along the horse

In early fall the water levels drop and slow, often warming the water, sparking some of the most consistent hatches of the year along with breathtaking scenery.

trail, we stopped at an overlook and could see trout moving in the gin-clear water 50 feet below our boots. Something was hatching but we didn't see any rises for another few hours when the sun finally broke through the clouds. The water warmed just enough to get the bugs and then the cutts moving. It also allowed me to shoot some photos even though the sun would usually go behind a cloud whenever I got my camera set up.

Toward mid-afternoon the light for photos was all but gone and Kerry and I focused on fishing techniques. She was very quick to learn new techniques and soon she was sticking trout on a regular basis. As the temperature dropped the small caddis and little yellow stones vanished and it was all over for the day. She ended with big smiles and knowing that she'd be back for more.

We had worked our way up to the horse bridge 3.2 miles into the Scapegoat. Just downstream there's a crossing for those horses and mules spooked by the bridge. We were wading across the river there and stopped to look upstream, admiring the bridge built so far from roads with many of the materials hauled in on horseback.

"Oh shit!" I said, grabbing the edge of Kerry's windbreaker.

"Oh shit what?" she asked, looking around for what had stopped me in mid-stride.

"Don't run and don't look directly into his face," I said, getting a bigger handful of her jacket.

The grizzly was running directly at us but kept looking over his shoulder. He wasn't charging, but that didn't relieve the pucker-factor I was experiencing. I lost sight of him for a moment and then he suddenly reappeared next to the bridge in full view, less than 30 yards away.

"Shit!" Kerry blurted out. I could feel her shiver ever so slightly, but her poise was so very impressive. "What do we do?"

"We don't run and we try to look like one large hombre," I answered, pulling her slightly toward me to show the bear a very large human with four legs.

He cocked his head once and then took off again at a gallop. The first few steps were toward us and I could feel Kerry pull slightly away.

"Don't run," I repeated as we stood our ground and watched the bear run up the other side of the hill slightly away from us.

"Now we move slowly away from him," I said. "Don't turn your back to him directly and don't run."

We moved slowly toward the horse trail on the side of the river away from the bear. Watching him with every step, I was

An angler can spend hours on the many long runs mixed in with stretches of riffles on the North Fork of the Blackfoot.

The concentration of spots near the tail is a visual identifier for cutthroats.

"He saw the bear," I said with a slight laugh. Even with a fully loaded packhorse and heavy rider they were moving at a pace that could have won a NASCAR event. Luckily we were already off the trail and as they went by Kerry asked, "Did you see the grizzly bear?"

"Yup," he replied. "Gotta go now."

In a second or two he was out of sight.

"Guess he doesn't much care for bears," I commented and then drank the rest of my water. I stuffed my waders into my pack and tightened my wet wading boots for the walk out.

There's a life-long bond that is formed when two people are threatened together by an out-side force. Kerry and I were now bonded. What a wonderful new friend I have.

The North Fork of the Blackfoot River will be my friend for life. Fishing a stream like this one isn't like fishing one of the big-name rivers. Fly fishers all over the world can plan their vacations around predictable hatch-es on waters like the Missouri, Madison, and Big Horn. The Trico hatch on the Missouri at the end of July is a given every year. But hatches and rising trout on streams like the North Fork are not something you can set your watch to, because each day the trig-ger will always be water temperature. Snowmelt, rain, cool weath-er, and even cloud cover can delay or even squash hatches. No hatches – no rising fish. It's the law of the North Fork.

The lower part of this 38-mile river is very floatable in canoes or inflatable rafts. One easy launch is at the Harry Morgan Fishing Access Site only a few miles from the town of Ovando. A short, two-mile float downriver takes you to the main stem of the Big Blackfoot River and the River Junction Campground. Here the North Fork brings new life to the Big B. Upstream, the Blackfoot slowly meanders and during summer months heats up to the temperature of bath water, but the cold water of the North Fork rescues the river, making it fit for all the downstream trout. Fishing this part of the river with any sort of dry fly before the

mentally preparing for Plan B if he decided to turn yet again and cross the river towards us. Ambling, he continued his trek up the hill and finally, finding some cover in the old deadfalls, slowed his pace and eventually stopped to peruse the situation. By this time we were well over 100 yards away and widening the gap with every step.

There are many old back woods sayings in Montana but one is "Never go into bear country with someone you can't outrun." I laughed about this as we briskly walked the trail while keeping track of the bear's location at all times. I'd come into grizzly bear country with a young marathon runner.

A half mile down the trail we stopped to retrieve her backpack and sat on a rock to take off our waders for the trek back to the campground. My senses were still on high alert and I heard the horse before I saw the riders. Kerry quickly turned when she saw my reaction and saw the first rider. He was pretty overweight and his horse was showing the strain. The guy had the cleanest cow-boy hat I'd ever seen and his eyes were open like someone trying to see their way through a dimly lit room.

Some faster moving sections of a stream, like this one on the North Fork of the Blackfoot, have small pockets of calm that hold fish.

temperature reaches around 50 degrees is mostly just casting practice. You can pick up some fish with weighed nymphs under an indicator, but be prepared for whitefish mania. Fortunately, on most summer days, the sun will do its job and both rivers are open for business by late morning.

Hatches of various species of mayflies, caddis, and stoneflies occur on this end of the river. Huge salmonflies can be gang-busters one year and elusive the next, but are always around to

The burn area on the hillside is a result of a fire that occurred in 1988.

some degree. Drakes, various caddis, and Little Yellow and Green Stoneflies are perennial favorites. While the Big B seems to be a buffet for hoppers and ants, the further upstream you travel on the North Fork, the fish are less inclined to take attractors or ter-restrials, unless those patterns closely mimic the current hatch. Then a pattern like a small Royal Wulff or Royal Trude may work. Keep in mind that the upwing and downwing patterns described in this book should be what populates the majority of your fly boxes. Carry the other patterns just because you always like to have them for that occasional experi-ment on a trout that holds in that little pool, flipping you the fin each time you drift another pattern over his head.

While there are many places to fish the lower end of the North Fork, most of it runs through private property and the very progressive "High Water Mark" law applies unless you receive permission from the landowner. Once you move upstream you'll find this river running through the Lolo National Forest with the headwaters of the North Fork in the Scapegoat Wilderness. Here, where the angler now has clear legal use of the river, you'll find some natural barriers.

Wilderness areas allow no mechanical use, including mountain bikes. While most anglers will walk the Hobnail Tom Trail adjacent to the river, it is also a well-used horse trail.

There are a few miles of fishable river from the North Fork Campground at the end of the road down-stream to where it enters private land. The first mile downstream from the campground to the bridge runs through a very steep canyon. I've climbed in and out of this canyon and it's not a trek for anyone in less-than-great health. Even then there are numerous dead falls, loose rocks, and extremely steep slopes. It is possible to start fishing at the bridge and fish upstream to the campground but this isn't for the feint of heart, as you'll spend much of your time rock climbing with your fly rod in one hand, trying to find a handhold with the other. The next mile downstream from the bridge is a little less intense.

The trailhead is at the north end of the campground. The trail is well established, pretty much obstacle-free, and easy to walk, but it doesn't give you easy jump-off access to the river in very many places. The first couple of miles taunt you because you can see the river far below and sometimes, with a good pair of polarized sunglasses, you can even see fish. The drop down to the river is steep and there is no guarantee that when you finally dip your felts into that cold, clear water there will be any fish rising.

At about mile 2.5 the trail gets within about 20 yards of the river for the first time and stays fairly close until it crosses the river at a horse bridge. My best calculation, aided by GPS, is that this is 3.15 trail miles from the campground. I have walked out the trail in 1.25 hours, but my pace has been described by some as a "death march."

Fishing this small river isn't really complex. The hatches are plentiful and varied but, as is typical in high mountain streams, you won't see blanket hatches of anything. Water temperature is the deciding factor. Below about 50 degrees, you will catch an occasional trout on nymph patterns like Peacock Soft Hackles, Hare's Ears, and Prince Nymphs. Before the water temperature triggers the hatch and thus the rising fish, you may choose to spend that time as I often do, munching on a granola bar and watching curious golden-mantled squirrels or river otters that have taken up residence here. These squirrels at first look like the typical chipmunk that's been fed a steady diet of steroids. They have the stripes of a chipmunk and the body mass of a fox squirrel. They are very curious and don't see many of the wadered crowd. The river otters are here also and do what otters do, which is chase fish and play.

The typical summer hatch on this river is often a simultaneous medley of two to sometimes six different aquatic insects, most of which can be mimicked with a Parachute Adams or a Deer Hair Caddis. The caddis pattern does a great job of fooling fish that are looking for the Little Yellow and Green Stoneflies. I tie and carry this pattern in both a ginger and olive color, but the ginger seems to fit the bill in 80 percent of situations. The natural insects vary from Gray Drakes and PMDs on the mayfly list, to Spotted Sedge, Grannom, and October Caddis on the caddis list. While any angler could easily narrow the fly selection to carry every needed pattern and size in one box, if you're like me you'll have about six boxes of flies just because you might find a time when something in the other boxes will work when nothing else will. I've fished these streams for a lot of years and I can count the number of times that something in those other boxes has worked on one hand. But yes, I still often carry them.

The North Fork isn't bewildering when it comes to figuring

Many different species of caddis are found on these streams. Some blend in with the substrate.

out where the fish will be holding. In water this cold they can't afford the caloric expense of fighting fast moving water while waiting for food to occasionally drift into their sight window. Instead, they hold in the slow to moderately moving water that gives them shelter from predators but also positions them for a chance to suck down lunch without a lot of work.

Westslope cutthroats are the predominant trout species on the upper river. They will take flies from the surface with abandon when a hatch is in full bloom. The takes are not the subtle, sippy type but more like a slap. One characteristic of these trout is that frequently they will take the fly on the way down. Patience is needed because fly fishers are used to quickly reacting when they see a snout breach the surface. It's more like hopper fishing when you should pause to allow the fish to take the fly and close his mouth around it. It takes the steely nerves of an NFL quarterback to wait until the time is right. When I'm on the river and hear an angler scream out, "I can't believe I missed him again," I know what the problem is because I've had to solve it myself many times. What great fun and joy this sport is because it is constantly challenging the angler to adapt to varying situations.

This upper section has mostly rock for structure, but you'll find many huge piles of wood debris that cutts love to hide under. The rocks are worn from centuries of water pounding against them and create wonderful current breaks for the fish. The wood debris is largely from a 250,000-acre fire in 1988.

In many places the water is so clear that you can see a fish rise from a great depth to take your fly. I miss most of these because I misjudge their speed and set the hook before the fish even takes it. This action on my part is normally followed by a heavy sigh and an "I can't believe I just did that – again!" Then I laugh and feel grateful that I'm fishing a remote stream where none of my old guide buddies are within earshot.

There aren't thousands of fish per river mile in this area because there will never be enough aquatic insects to support a high density of fish. The fish here endure very long and harsh winters. That ten-inch cutt you just released has lived more years than a trout twice his size on a pampered tailwater. Carefully releasing these beautiful high-country marvels must be the

The lower North Fork is large enough to support fishing from rafts, but wading is also an option.

order of the day. Smash your barbs to quicken the process. Each trout you catch is a rare jewel, regardless of size, and should be treated with great respect and care. These are not the common hatchery rainbows that populate most of the trout streams across America. Rather, they are a fish with an uncertain future, found only in the wilds of a fraction of the streams of our country. Treat them like the treasures they are.

Fishing downstream has certain advantages. Your drifts tend to be more drag free and the fish aren't spooked by fly line and leader over their heads. However, there are several distinct disadvantages, the first being that feeding fish are always looking upstream so your profile needs to be very low to stay out of their sight. My biggest problem is that when you kick up debris from wading, it drifts right into the fish you are trying to catch. Often this will put fish down because of the muddy water or just because debris floats by them.

Fishing upstream eliminates both of these problems. The only thing needed is more careful presentations and delicate landings. The rising trout I've encountered don't seem put off by a leader on the surface of their feeding lane, but most are going to be at least a little spooked by more than a couple of feet of fly line passing over their heads. The solution is short, accurate casts that show them only the leader and fly. Careful stalking of these active surface feeders will pay off big time and haste will only put fish down, so slow, deliberate movements are key. If you watch a heron move in the water, you've got a great role model to mimic.

When a hatch begins, the predominant species of westslope cutthroats will move into pools like this one to feed.

CHAPTER NINE

Copper Creek
Burn Areas

*F*ire! In the Rocky Mountain West that one word awakens a primal fear in anyone who has lived here longer than a few years. From 2000 through 2003, over two million acres of forest burned in Montana alone. That's roughly half the size of Massachusetts.

There are remnants of old burns all over the West and all the big ones have names. During drought years their smoke fills the skies for months and residents cough the particulates out of their lungs long after the autumn snows finally extinguish the fires and clean the air.

In the summer of 2003, the Snow Talon Fire on upper Copper Creek was such a fire. It was started by either a careless camper or by lightning. There were tent cities east of the town of Lincoln along the Big Blackfoot River. When the snows finally came and the smoke cleared in late September, it was a relief. Even though this fire was about 30 miles from my house, I knew the area well and each time I drove through on Highway 200 it seemed like the faces of the firefighters looked more and more defeated.

It wasn't until the next spring that I was able to venture into the area to see the damage for myself. It was truly a changed landscape. Nearly 60 square miles of blackened trees stretched to the horizon. Bridges had burned and were pulled out by heavy equipment so that no one would be

Recently burned Copper Creek looks pretty bleak in some areas, but other sections seem to be untouched by the devastation. The trout population didn't seem to suffer from the fire.

foolish enough to venture over them. Metal signs were melted on the ground amid piles of charred timbers. All the campgrounds were closed although the Forest Service toilets seemed to have escaped damage, which was amazing since there were cooked trees within an arm's reach of them.

The first signs of fish life I saw were risers on Snowbank Lake. The fish didn't seem to notice that the landscape had changed. There were small mayflies coming off and a little Parachute Adams fooled the occasional cutt, but this was still early and the smaller, more vulnerable Lovebug dropped off the Adams won the contest hands down. None of the cutts were very big, but it gave me hope that the fire hadn't devastated the stream itself.

At first I thought that other fly fishers had the same curiosity as I had, as there were several vehicles driving up and down the road through the middle of the burned area. Then I saw the white buckets – 'shroomers! More specifically, they were on the hunt for morel mushrooms that seem to flourish in the mineral-rich areas of recent burns. Since dried morel mushrooms retail for around the same price as diamonds, don't be surprised if you see platoons of fungus finders around streams that have seen recent burns.

After driving around for a time, I finally had to investigate the substrate of the stream. I knew if the aquatic insect life was missing, there wasn't much chance of catching any trout. What I found was amazing. Instead of silted water and a sterile bottom, the stream was running silt-free and clear and there were caddis on almost every rock. A closer inspection found several species of mayflies and stoneflies. Life had found a way.

The fishing was sporadic until July when the weather and water finally warmed up. There were a couple of times when the road was washed out because of the lack of trees and vegetation to hold back the spring rains, but in the end this small stream fished almost as well as it had in previous years, but without the summer campers who were barred from the closed campgrounds.

It was somewhat eerie working my way through the blackened earth and trees, occasionally finding a remnant of the battle like a piece of burnt fire hose or a burned-out bridge. Then I heard it, the distinct sound of a rise. Turning to the sound, I froze, waiting for the fish to surface again. It surprised me to see him so close and downstream of my position. Slowly, I turned away from the stream and headed into the cover of the trees, making a big loop to approach him from downstream.

By the time I'd gotten into position, he had two enthusiastic friends taking the small

Copper Creek

LEGEND

Highway	
Gravel Road	
River	
Campground	Λ
Bridge	)(
City	⊙
Trailhead	🚶
Public Land	
Private Land	

Copper Creek

Indian Meadows Campground

Copper Creek Campground

Snowbank Lake

Copper Creek Road

Copper Creek

Landers Fork

Landers Fork

Landers Fork Road

To Rogers Pass

200

279

To Helena

To Lincoln

200

Blackfoot River

N

Miles   0   1   2   3

One benefit from the fire was that it allowed more sunlight to warm the substrate. This increased the population of aquatic insects.

Additional deadfalls caused by the fire provide shelter for the trout, but care must be taken when walking among some of these fire-weakened trees.

caddis from the surface near a pile of wood debris. While tying on the small Deer Hair Caddis, I noticed that my hands were trembling. Maybe it was that third cup of coffee mixed with just the right amount of adrenaline, but it took me a minute to get the tippet through the moving target of the hook eye. Taking a deep breath I exhaled with a laugh. My first cast was just off target and floated into a little eddy, unnoticed by the rising trout. The second cast was perfect and landed right on the seam, just upstream of the snouts. Gently it floated toward the target, turning first left and then slightly right. A head breached the surface and took my imitation without any hesitation. As I set the hook I could feel the mass. The trout responded by quickly seeking the sanctuary of the pile of wood and tree roots. I countered with pressure from my rod tip, directing him into the middle of the stream. He darted through the hole and the other fish responded by quickly swimming away from an unknown threat.

As he finally came to hand I marveled at the beauty of this water-borne creature. The telltale gill slash told me it was a westslope cutthroat. Instead of picking up the fish, I simply grabbed my barbless fly and turned it backwards, freeing the fish to return, no doubt slightly puzzled, to the security of the wood.

For the next four hours or so I found myself immersed in this wonderland. The hatch was in full bloom and the fish were waiting for the flies at each turn of the creek. My hands stopped trembling as I adjusted to this gift of opportunity, and for a time I was the only human on the earth. ꙮ

Some sections of Copper Creek show the full brunt of the fire's devastation, but on closer look you see the new growth on the forest floor.

CHAPTER TEN

Patterns

When faced with a new challenge, I have several strategies, but the one that works best when I have a fly rod in my hand is adaptation. Often, methods or techniques that served you well on one stream will serve you well on another as long as the environments aren't too different.

If this method fails, steal ideas shamelessly from anyone you can.

After fishing the Missouri River for several years it was apparent that a transition fly was needed to fill the gap between deep nymphs and dry flies. Many hours passed with me sitting on the bank or in my drift boat watching fish take natural insects. My little binoculars became part of my face. Then there were the hours spent standing in the river with a seine trying to capture what food the fish had keyed on. There were many discoveries from this research that led me to change many of my fly patterns as well as the way I instructed clients to fish them.

The Lovebug emerged as an instantaneous winner. The niche was filled with this wonderful little pattern that easily mimicked a trigger for the trout. The fish were looking for a small profile that was highly segmented and vulnerable looking. Soon I had other guides asking me for this pattern that was versatile enough to fish deep as a nymph as well as a transitional fly that mimicked the stage just before emergence. Normally we would drop it off a dry fly pattern.

The average fly fisher needs about 10 fly patterns. He will carry another 100 or so for the off chance he will encounter that one picky fish.

My friend and fellow guide Dan Gard approached me in the Missouri River Trout Shop parking lot one morning as we both waited for our clients. We were finishing off that last cup of coffee, ready for the day ahead. Dan is a very outgoing guy with a sense of humor that seems to know no taboos. He's one of the most generous guides I know with his flies, information, and materials.

I was loading my lunches into the coolers as he approached. I could smell his cherry flavored cigars before he even spoke and it was obvious he was a man with a head full of questions.

"Hey buddy. I saw your clients killing 'em yesterday. Have you got some sort of Hoover vacuum cleaner in that boat of yours? My guys really didn't do very well and your guys seemed to always have a fish on. What were ya' using?"

I couldn't resist the opportunity. "Well, Dan, first off, they were using a better guide." We both busted up laughing.

"No, seriously, spill your guts, dude. I tried everything I could think of and nothing really worked very well." He was ready to bargain now as he was facing another day on the river with the same clients who would be asking him the same questions.

"These," I said as I held out my hand. Dan quickly threw down his cigar and ground it into the parking lot gravel while reaching for his free lottery tickets.

"Cool," he said. "Yeah, I can see why these would work. Do you fish them deep or dropped off a dry fly?"

"Either way," I replied, closing the cooler. "I made it for the transition, but they seem to work just as well as a deep nymph."

Dan was looking at the flies like an old prospector that had just hit the mother lode. He thanked me and promised he would keep the pattern a secret. He kept promising over and over to never tell another soul. Later that day, his boat was just behind a film crew shooting an ESPN fishing show. Kurt Gowdy and his son were later shown enjoying the many pleasures of the Missouri River. Dan was not part of this film project, but finding himself on the same stretch of river, he positioned his boat and clients so as not to interfere, even though that meant following them down the river.

He guided his clients along a normally productive bank above the Craig bridge and one of his guys hooked and finally landed a 26-inch brown that Dan later described as the size of a small sea lion. His client had caught it on one of the Lovebugs I'd given Dan that morning.

Mammoth trout stories spread like wind-driven snowstorms across the Montana high country. The question, "What fly did he eat?" isn't the first question, because that would be considered rude, but it soon works its way into the conversation.

Dan probably hesitated for a moment because his conscience would tingle as he remembered the promise he'd made to me about keeping the pattern a secret. But his silence was about as likely as him holding his bowels after eating a bushel of prunes. Within days everyone in our solar system knew about the Lovebug.

A few days later while guiding some other clients, I stopped at the top end of an island to eat lunch. As we were enjoying our meal and reminiscing about the great morning of fishing, two anglers approached on foot. Both appeared to be in their mid-20s and it was obvious from their laughter and demeanor that they were having a great day on the river.

"How's it going gentlemen?" I queried as they neared us.

"We're having the time of our life," one replied. "We've never had a day like this."

"That's great," I said. "I'm always happy to see people enjoy themselves."

"How are you guys doing?" He asked but it was apparent that he had something he wanted to tell us. Before any of us could answer he was blurting it out.

"We've just been killing them on this one fly," he said, looking around to make sure no one else was listening to this conversation.

"We fished with a guide yesterday and he gave us a few. It's a secret fly that no one else on the river has ever used before." He had my interest and as he opened his fly box, I saw the secret fly immediately but I remained silent, hoping my grin wouldn't ruin his moment of glory.

"Here it is," he declared, holding up the fly like he was offering the Holy Grail to the King.

"It's a secret. It's called a..." My client cut him off and finished his sentence with "Lovebug." The angler looked as if he'd been gut shot.

"What the...how did you know that?" He couldn't believe what he was hearing.

My client then reached over and took a fly box from my vest, opened it, and displayed several neat and orderly rows of the secret pattern.

"But Dan Gard told us that a buddy of his named Trapper came up with this pattern and no one else on the river even knew about it." His voice was full of despair.

"He's Trapper," said my client, pointing to me. He was really enjoying this more than he should have but it was humorous. He then returned his attention to polishing off his chocolate cake.

"Wow, well let me just tell you that this is a great pattern and I won't tell anyone about it. I promise." It was a lie before it ever left his mouth.

"Don't worry about it," I said. "Look, you have my permission to tell anyone you like about this fly. You're going to anyway, so you might as well have a clear conscience about it. That's what fly fishing is supposed to be about – people having fun in a non-competitive environment." ✑

Catching trout with flies you've tied adds a new dimension to fly fishing. Modifying existing patterns or creating your own patterns is also very rewarding.

Dry Fly Patterns

LaFontaine Caddis Emerger

Hook: TMC 100, 101
  (dry fly hook)
Size: 16-18
Thread: 8/0 Olive
Trailing shuck: Tan Antron
Underbody: Olive Antron
  dubbing
Overbody: Tan Antron yarn
Emergent Wing: Deer or
  elk hair
Collar: Brown ostrich herl

Parachute Adams

Hook: TMC 100, 101
  (dry fly hook)
Size: 12-20
Thread: 8/0 Gray
Tail: Brown and grizzly
  hackle, shank length
Body: Beaver - Adams gray
Post: White Antron
Parachute Wing: Brown
  and grizzly hackle

Deer Hair Caddis

Hook: TMC 100, 101
  (dry fly hook)
Size: 16-18
Thread: 8/0 Tan
Body: Light brown Hare's
  Ear dubbing
Hackle: Barred ginger
Rib: Thread
Wing: Whitetail deer hair

CDC Parachute

Hook: TMC 100, 101
  (dry fly hook)
Size: 16-18
Thread: 8/0 Tan
Tail: Wood Duck
Body: Ginger biot
Post: White CDC
Thorax: Light brown
  Hare's Ear
Parachute Wing: Barred
  ginger

PMD Cripple

Hook: TMC 100, 101
  (Dry fly hook)
Size: 16-18
Thread: 8/0 Brown
Tail: Pheasant Tail
Body: Pheasant Tail
Rib: Gold wire
Thorax: Yellow Hare/
  Antron dubbing
Wing: Coastal Deer Hair
Hackle: Barred light ginger

Capture and then closely study the resident aquatic insects like this Caddisfly.

Nymph Patterns

Lovebug

Hook: 2x short, 2x heavy Scud hook TMC 2457

Size: 18 – 20

Bead: 2mm or 18, 1.5 mm for 20

Thread: 8/0 Iron gray or dark gray

Tail: A single strand of tinsel, shank length

Underbody: Iron gray thread

Body: Stripped grizzly hackle stem

Rib: Fine gold wire

Thorax: Natural beaver

Emergent Wing: Hungarian partridge

Prince Nymph

Hook: 2x short, 2x heavy Scud hook TMC 2457

Size: 16 – 18

Bead: 2mm

Thread: 8/0 Olive

Tail: Goose biot, white

Body: Peacock herl

Rib: Gold wire

Wing: Goose biot, white

Collar: Hungarian partridge

Peacock Soft Hackle

Hook: 2x short, 2x heavy Scud hook TMC 2457

Size: 16 – 18

Bead: 2mm

Thread: 8/0 Olive

Tail: Olive micro fibbets

Body: Peacock herl

Rib: Gold wire

Wing: Hungarian partridge

Flashback Hare's Ear

Hook: 2x short, 2x heavy Scud hook TMC 2457

Size: 16 – 18

Bead: 2mm

Thread: 8/0 Tan

Tail: Hungarian partridge

Body: Light brown Hare's Ear with 20% tan Antron dubbing

Rib: Gold wire

Thorax: Light brown Hare's Ear with 20% tan Antron dubbing

Wing case: Krystal flash

When choosing a pattern, start with the size and profile of the naturals you capture.

Afterword

It is now mid-winter here in western Montana. The temperature is minus 15 degrees and a blanket of snow has buried my picnic table. The other big lump out there is the grill that I had made a mental note to put in the shed before it started snowing. My DirectTV dish is the only thing free of snow because it hangs under the eave of my house.

Stamping the snow from my feet, I carry an armload of fir through the house to the wood stove. As I open the stove door, the ice in my beard melts and splatters on the hot metal, dancing momentarily before it vanishes in a vapor wisp. The frozen wood I throw into the firebox steams and sizzles as it hits the hot coals, and I quickly close the door to prevent the popping embers from escaping.

The heat from the stove soothes me as I plop my butt down in the rocker and pick up the remote. The NFL playoff games that come into my living room via the satellite dish are amazing with their digital sound and image.

Calling my friends and family while out in the middle of nowhere on my cell phone keeps me in touch when I'm out late on the river and need to tell Shirley that I'll be late and she needn't worry.

Using Microsoft Word software on my computer is much easier than a type-writer or pencil. Being able to email photos of my grandsons to friends is really a tremendous convenience. And checking river flows off the USGS website has saved me countless hours and heartache.

But stock portfolios don't teach me what is important in life. I can't find the answers to the really profound questions by using Internet search engines. While I certainly enjoy these technological marvels, they tend to starve me of what I really hunger for.

Fly fishing small streams in the solitude of Montana gives me more joy than I probably deserve. In our high-tech world of communication satellites and wireless Internet connections, I find myself yearning for the simplicity of these isolated places. Here, the chaotic buzz of millions of people talking on cell phones is silenced by the buzz of a single caddisfly that is hopelessly stuck between my eye-lashes and sunglasses.

These are simple, quiet places where a fly fisher can lose the entire universe except for that small piece of real estate between him and the trout. This elegant endeavor puts me into a state of mind where all sounds are silenced except the harmony of my fly line as it floats through the air on the way to the water. This down-to-earth endeavor teaches me what life is about and why I am here on this small, blue, water planet.

My soul is blissfully bonded to these waters. ⌐